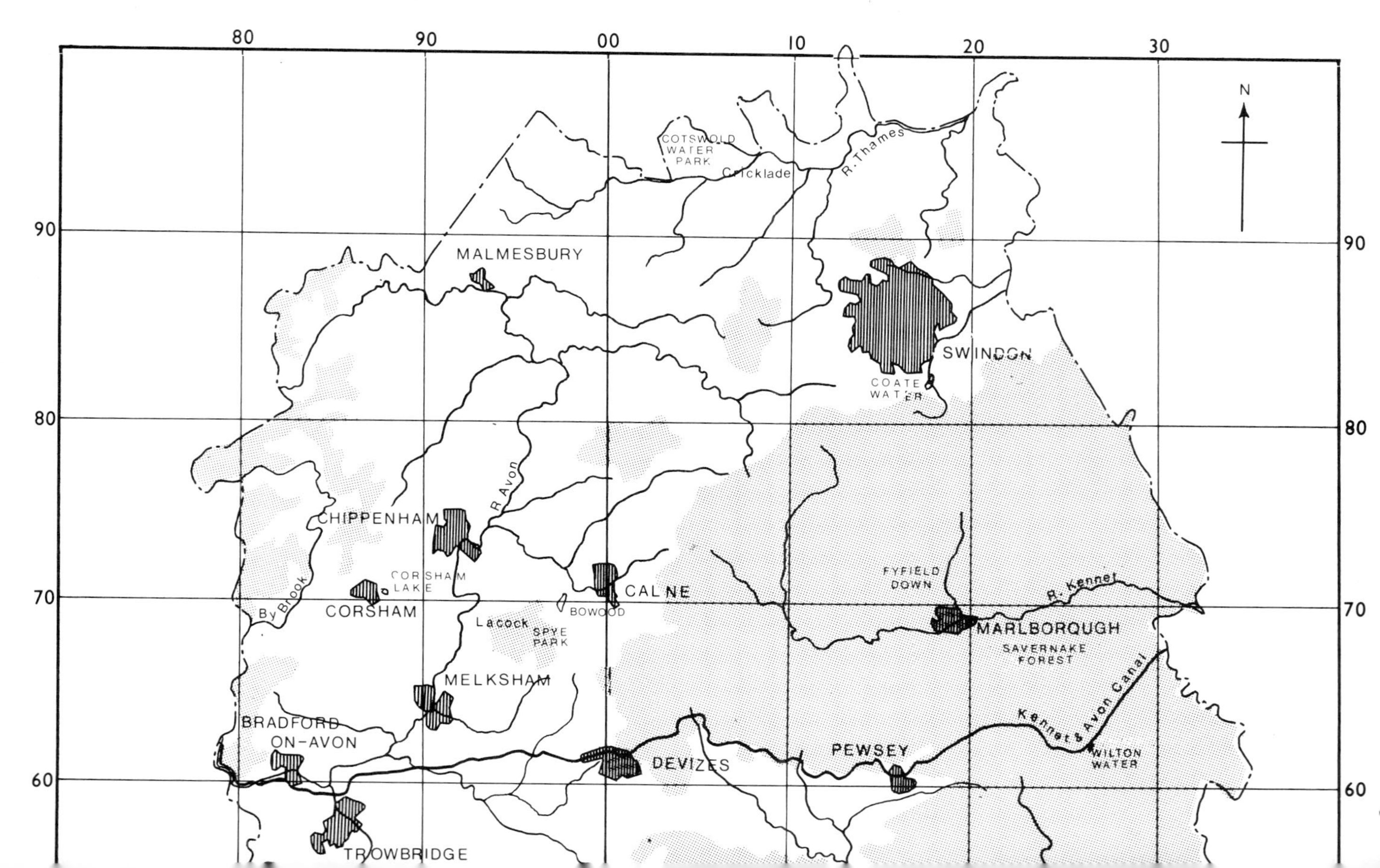
N
MALMESBURY
COTSWOLD WATER PARK
Cricklade
R. Thames
SWINDON
COATE WATER
CHIPPENHAM
R Avon
CORSHAM LAKE
CORSHAM
By Brook
CALNE
BOWOOD
Lacock
SPYE PARK
FYFIELD DOWN
R. Kennet
MARLBOROUGH
SAVERNAKE FOREST
Kennet & Avon Canal
WILTON WATER
MELKSHAM
BRADFORD ON-AVON
DEVIZES
PEWSEY
TROWBRIDGE
80
90
00
10
20
30
60
70

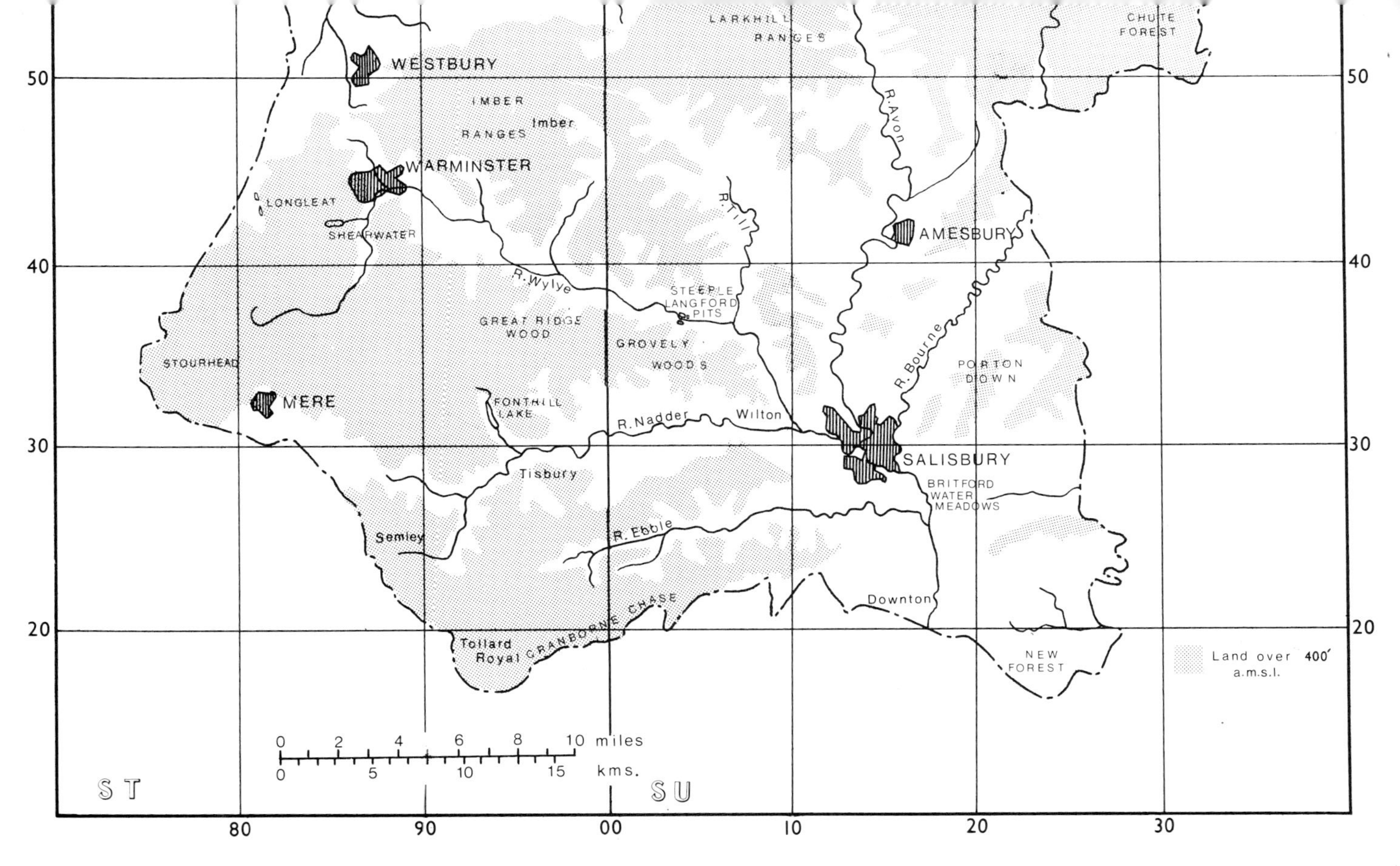
LARKHILL
RANGES
CHUTE
FOREST
WESTBURY
IMBER
RANGES
Imber
WARMINSTER
LONGLEAT
SHEARWATER
R.Avon
R.Till
AMESBURY
R.Wylye
STEEPLE
LANGFORD
PITS
GREAT RIDGE
WOOD
GROVELY
WOODS
STOURHEAD
R.Bourne
PORTON
DOWN
MERE
FONTHILL
LAKE
R.Nadder
Wilton
SALISBURY
BRITFORD
WATER
MEADOWS
Tisbury
Semley
R.Ebble
CRANBORNE CHASE
Downton
Tollard
Royal
NEW
FOREST
Land over 400′
a.m.s.l.
0 2 4 6 8 10 miles
0 5 10 15 kms.
ST
SU
50
40
30
20
80
90
00
10
20
30

THE BIRDS OF WILTSHIRE

THE BIRDS OF WILTSHIRE

Edited for

The Wiltshire Ornithological Society

by

John Buxton, MA, MBOU

Trowbridge

Wiltshire Library & Museum Service

1981

Published by Wiltshire Library & Museum Service
Director: Frederick Hallworth, OBE, FLA, FRGS
for

Designed by Edward J. Kelly, ALA
Printed by John Wright & Sons Ltd at the Stonebridge Press, Bath Road Brislington Bristol BS4 5NU
ISBN 0 86080 080 6

Dedicated to the memory of

Ruth Barnes

(1901–1981)

first president of

The Wiltshire Ornithological Society

CONTENTS

LIST OF ILLUSTRATIONS

The vignettes illustrating the Systematic List were drawn by John Govett.

ACKNOWLEDGEMENTS

The thanks of The Wiltshire Ornithological Society are due to Mr. Charles Bridgman for re-typing much of the book from the corrected drafts; to Mr. Geoffrey Stone for assistance to the Editor and liaison with the publisher; and to the following for information supplied to the writers of various sections of the book:

A. Baker
H.M. Dobinson
S.B. Edwards
Mrs. B. Fergusson
D.T. Paradise
F.G. Parsons
A.M. Rackham
J.C. Rolls
E.P. Stephens
J.A. Stevenson
D. Walker
Mrs. J.E. Wilder

The Society also wishes to thank the Director of Wiltshire Library & Museum Service, Mr. Frederick Hallworth, for allowing this book to be issued as part of the Service's publishing programme.

PREFACE

The Wiltshire Ornithological Society was founded on 30 November, 1974, and on 3 December, 1976, the Executive Committee set up a sub-committee to undertake the preparation of the *The Birds of Wiltshire*. This sub-committee had its first meeting on 21 January, 1977, and invited me to serve as editor. The previous handlist, edited by L.G. Peirson, was published by the Natural History Section of the Wiltshire Archaeological and Natural History Society in 1959, and a Supplement, edited by G.L. Webber, was published by the same Society in 1968.

The present volume is intended to bring information up to date to the end of 1979, with a few records of unusual interest from 1980. It includes brief accounts of different regions of the county (whose boundaries were fortunately left undisturbed in the recent reorganization which damaged so many of the neighbouring counties) written by members of the Society with personal knowledge of these.

Place-names are given in the form preferred by the editors of *The Place-names of Wiltshire*, (English Place-name Society, vol. XVI) 1939.

The photographs, intended to show a variety of habitats, were specially taken for the book by Mr E.C. Deadman, Mr. G.A. Maclean and Mr. M.H. Smith, to whom the thanks of the Wiltshire Ornithological Society are due.

We are also grateful to Dr. Ennion and to the Council of the Wiltshire Trust for Nature Conservation for permitting us to use his drawing of a Hobby as the front cover illustration.

East Tytherton — John Buxton
October 1980

A

DISCOURSE

ON THE

Emigration of Britiſh Birds:

OR,

This QUESTION at laſt SOLV'D:

Whence come the STORK and the TURTLE, the CRANE and the SWALLOW, when they know and obſerve the appointed Time of their coming?

CONTAINING

A curious, particular, and circumſtantial ACCOUNT of the reſpective Retreats of all thoſe

BIRDS of PASSAGE

Which viſit our Iſland at the Commencement of SPRING, and depart at the Approach of WINTER; as, the

CUCKOW,	The SWALLOW TRIBE,	WHIN-CHAT,
TURTLE,	NIGHTINGALE,	WILLOW-WREN,
STORK,	BLACK-CAP,	WHITE-THROAT,
CRANE,	WHEAT-EAR,	ETOTOLI,
QUAIL,	STONE-CHAT,	FLY-CATCHER,
GOAT-SUCKER,		&c. &c.

ALSO,

A copious, entertaining, and ſatisfactory Relation of

WINTER BIRDS of PASSAGE,

Among which are the

WOODCOCK,	FIELDFARE,	ROYSTON CROW,
SNIPE,	RED-WING,	DOTTEREL, &c.

SHEWING

The different Countries to which they retire, the Places where they breed, and how they perform their Annual Emigrations, &c.

With a ſhort Account of thoſe BIRDS that migrate occaſionally, or only ſhift their Quarters at certain Seaſons of the Year.

To which are added,

REFLECTIONS on that truly admirable and wonderful Inſtinct, the ANNUAL MIGRATION of BIRDS!

By a NATURALIST.

SALISBURY:
Printed and ſold by COLLINS and JOHNSON,
For the AUTHOR.
Sold alſo by FIELDING and WALKER, in Pater-noſter Row, London,
M DCC LXXX,

WILTSHIRE ORNITHOLOGISTS

by Ruth Barnes

WHEN considering those ornithologists, who either by birth or their work and writings can be claimed for Wiltshire, no less a personage than John Aubrey (1626-1697) author of the now well-known *Brief Lives* appears to be the earliest, but his notes, made between 1656 and 1691, which comprise *The Natural History of Wiltshire,* were not printed until 1847 when they were edited by John Britton for the Wiltshire Topographical Society. Aubrey was born at Easton Piercy and educated at Malmesbury Grammar School and Trinity College, Oxford. He was a student of the Middle Temple but was never called to the Bar.

Apart from references to hawks and hawking his chapter on Birds amounts to one and a half pages and A.C. Smith did not think much of them, magisterially commenting in his *Birds of Wiltshire* "as regards ornithology he was ludicrously ill-informed even for that unscientific age" and "He contrives to embody quite as many errors as facts".

Reference is made to buntings, linnets and woodpeckers, "a great plenty of larks, especially in Colern-fields and those parts adjoining the Cotswolds. They take them by alluring them with a daring glasse, which is whirled about on a sun shining day, and the larks are pleased at it . . . while he whistles with his larke-call of silver. In the south part of Wiltshire they catch these pretty aetheriall birds with trammells. In Sir James Long's park at Draycot Cerne are some wheat-eares, and on conie warrens and downes but not in great plenty. . . It is a great delicacie, and they are little lumps of fat. On Salisbury Plaines especially about Stonehenge are bustards, they are also in the fields above Lavington. They do not often come to Chalke. On Salisbury Plaines are grey crows as at Royston. Bitterns in the breaches at Allington. Herons bred heretofore about 1580 at Easton Piercy before the great oaks were felled down near the mannour house. An eerie of sparrow-hawkes at the park at

Kington St. Michael. The hobbies doe goe away and return at the spring. Quaerie Sir James Long if any other hawke doe the like? Sea-mewes. Plenty of them at Colerne-downe; elsewhere in Wiltshire I doe not remember them."

He wrote that in the days before the dissolution of the monasteries "every yeoman once kept a sparrow hawk, every priest a hobie".

George Montagu (1751-1815) son of James Montagu and Elizabeth, daughter of William Hedges of Alderton, was born at Lackham House, a building later destroyed by fire and rebuilt. He joined the Army at the age of sixteen and at nineteen went to fight in the war of the American Colonies and was promoted captain in the 15th Regt. of Foot. While in America he began to collect birds. He was an early member of the Linnaean Society for which he wrote papers. He married at the age of eighteen Anne, daughter of William and Lady Jane Courtenay and lived for some time at Easton Grey and then at Alderton House, which he shared with his mother-in-law. When inheritance enabled him to resign from the Wiltshire Militia he moved to Kingsbridge in Devon, where he spent the rest of his life. After his death the British Museum on the advice of Sir Joseph Banks bought his collection of birds and other animals for £1,200.

He first described the Grey Phalarope from one killed on a pond at Alderton and in his Dictionary first noted the difference between the Hen Harrier and the bird still known as the Montagu's Harrier after him. He added the Little White Heron (Cattle Egret), Red-breasted Snipe, Little Gull, Roseate Tern and Cirl Bunting to the British list. He proved that the Scaup was sexually dimorphic. (It had previously been thought that the duck and drake were two species.) He also described several new species of fish, molluscs and worms.

He published his *Ornithological Dictionary of British Birds* in 1802. Max Nicholson in *Birds in England* refers to him as "one of the most knowledgeable writers of modern times, his accuracy and precision when he writes from his own knowledge is almost miraculous." A.C. Smith called him "one of the most acute observers and one of the most reliable authors of his age" and said "one giant we have had among us, the eminent ornithologist Colonel Montagu."

Of Wiltshire birds A.C. Smith quotes Montagu as saying

"that the Grasshopper Warbler is nowhere so plentiful as on Malmesbury Common to which the males come about the latter end of April".

He recorded much that interests us today: life history and change of plumage by sex, age and season. He also invalidated several species which were wrongly identified. He corresponded with the Rev. Gilbert White of Selborne in Hampshire whose *Natural History* of that village is still read and enjoyed. Unfortunately, due to the unattractive way in which Montagu's work is presented, both book and distinguished author are today almost unknown.*

The initials, "J.L, Market Lavington" preserved the anonymity of the writer of *A Discourse on the Emigration of British Birds* for a century until, prompted by enquiries from Professor Alfred Newton, the Rev. A.C. Smith made a search and found the marble tablet in the church of Market Lavington to John Legg, who died in 1802 aged 47. Smith then published in the *Wiltshire Archaeological Magazine* for December 1894 some family history of "this advanced ornithologist of the 18th Century". Two editions of the *Discourse* were printed in Salisbury in 1780, a third in 1795, and a fourth in London in 1814 when the printer substituted the name of the then well known ornithologist George Edwards, no doubt to increase sales.

John Legg led a secluded life and died young. *The History of British Birds* which he claims to have written was never published and has never been found. The *Discourse* refutes the theories that birds spend the winter hibernating in a torpid state in holes in trees and buildings, or under ice at the bottom of lakes, or that they fly to the moon. He supports the arguments for migration and he probably made the first systematic observations in Wiltshire of migrants. He wrote of Swallows "I find by my journal that they appeared in Wiltshire on April 5th,

---

**Ornithological Dictionary*, published in London 1802; a Supplement at Exeter 1813; 2nd edition with articles by James Rennie 1831; reprinted 1866 as a *Dictionary of British Birds* edited by E. Newman, the editor of the *Zoologist* who re-wrote almost the whole work and incorporated additional species; a later edition by Sonnenschein and Allen is undated. *A Biographical Sketch of Col. George Montagu 1751-1815, English Field Zoologist,* by Bruce Cummings, Zoological Dept. British Museum, *Zoologische Annalen* 1912. Article by Wm. Cunnington *Wiltshire Archaeological Magazine* 1857.

1774, and disappeared on the 9th of October. In 1775 they were seen on April 3rd, and left us October the 14th. In 1776 on the 7th of April, and left us a day later (than in 1775). In the space of five revolving seasons, the time of their arrival and disappearing agreed almost to a day. . . The different species of swallows do not go and come at the same time, the Sand Martin usually arrives first; about a week after, the Swallow is seen; a few days later, Common Martins come in great numbers." He also refers to records of swallows seen at sea and alighting exhausted on ships. "Extraordinary as it may appear, it is certain that the Swift constantly disappears about the middle of August."

We might claim that he was the first to attempt bird marking for identification and so the forerunner of Wiltshire bird ringers. "Flycatchers I have known to build eight, nine and even ten years successively in a certain crevice of an old wall, not far from my dwelling: apprehensive that it was the same bird which annually and invariably visited the spot, curiosity prompted me to try an experiment, which put the matter out of doubt. When an opportunity offered, I took the female, cut off the extremity of the upper mandible of the bill, and with a knife made several perspicuous marks on its claws; this done, I set her at liberty; the succeeding spring the same bird returned, with the distinguishing marks I had given it, which was at once satisfactory. Perhaps some will say it is impossible the bird should survive, after it was deprived of the point of its bill; they will, however, please to observe that what was cut was so very inconsiderable, that the loss of it could hardly be perceptible to the bird; it could not therefore be any way detrimental to its feeding."

An interesting note is one on the Dotterel; "it is only a wanderer, shifting its habitation in the vernal and autumnal season from the marshes to hilly situations. At those times they are very common on the Wiltshire and Berkshire downs."

His *Natural History of the Nightingale* in the *Ladies Magazine or Entertaining Companion for the Fair Sex,* shows an intimate knowledge of this bird's nesting habits and perhaps even more of practical advice for keeping Nightingales in captivity and on their diet, interspersed with lines from Pliny, Milton and Thomson.*

*There was reference to Legg in *The Zoologist* 1904 and correspondence in *Notes and Queries* between 1904 and 1914; an article in the Naturalists' Column in *The*

William George Maton, M.D., F.R.S., F.R.C.P., F.L.S., F.S.A., (1774-1835) was educated at the Grammar School, Salisbury and Queen's College, Oxford and trained at Westminster Hospital. He practised in Weymouth during the season. A youthful naturalist, he discovered a new Tellina (*T. nivalis*, a cockle-like bivalve) in the Salisbury Avon and was elected Fellow of the Linnaean Society at the age of 20. His little book *The Natural History of a Part of the County of Wilts Comprehended within the distance of ten miles round the city of Salisbury* was not published until 1843, after his death. This contained 55 pages Vegetabilia, four pages Aves, one page Amphibia, one page Pisces, two pages Vermes.

Twenty-three species of birds are listed with very brief notes, chosen solely for personal reasons. The only bird of prey mentioned is the Kite "seen sometimes about Downton". He bought Redlynch House shortly before his death and discovered Asarabacca (*Asarum europaeum,* a plant of the Birthwort family) there. Some rarities had been shot: Hoopoe and Wryneck. "The Blackbird is much detested by gardeners." In a footnote "The Bustard was an inhabitant of Plain but the writer believes that one might as successfully look for an Ostrich there in the present . . . not only has cultivation closely gained upon the haunts of this bird and thus curtailed him of his appropriate food but human habitations have also disturbed his solitude. A very observant and credible person of the name of Dew, whom I knew as a sportsman in my younger days, informed me in the year 1796, that he once saw as many as seven or eight of these birds together on the Downs, near Winterbourne Stoke, but I have not met with anyone since who has actually seen the bustard in Wiltshire subsequently to that year."

A.C. Smith wrote of Maton "anything more meagre and more absolutely misleading on account of its wholesale omissions than the wretched account he gives of Wiltshire birds it is impossible to conceive".

Field Feb. 1918 and another in *British Birds* XVII, by Sir Hugh Gladstone. Curiosity was aroused by the name "etotoli" or "etoboli" concluding the list of species on the title page of the *Discourse*: it was suggested that it was a printer's error for "et alii" ("and others") or etcetera. Legg also published *A New Treatise on the Art of Grafting and Inoculation by an Experienced Practitioner in this branch of Gardening.*

The Rev. George Thomas Marsh (1812-1862) spent his childhood in Winterslow. He was appointed Vicar of Sutton Benger in 1836, rebuilt the Parsonage in 1841 and restored the church in 1849. He resigned the living in 1861 and died of consumption in Nice at the age of 49 the following year. His parishioners filled a three-light window with stained glass in his memory. The Editor of *British Birds* sent the present writer a proof copy of a letter from William E. Glegg published in March 1956 in which he refers to an interleaved copy, signed and dated 5th August 1842, of Yarrell's *History of British Birds* in which Marsh had made notes. The book is now in the library of the Bird Room of the British Museum, Natural History, at Tring. Glegg writes "The notes deal chiefly with the status of birds in Wilts but Mr. Marsh was a keen collector and did not confine his attention to Wilts. On his death his collection passed to his brother Mr. Matthew Marsh and on the death of the latter to South Wilts Museum, Salisbury. Although the Rev. A.C. Smith does not refer to the annotated copy, he made use of Mr. Marsh's notes for his *Birds of Wiltshire* 1887. When any further work on the birds of Wiltshire is undertaken this annotated copy should not be overlooked".

A.C. Smith refers to Marsh as "my very intimate and deeply lamented friend, a thoroughly practical ornithologist whose ear was so accurate and whose knowledge of birds from long personal observation was so profound." Marsh noted 157 species as occurring in the county. Some are rarities such as the White-tailed Eagle caught in a trap in Braydon Forest in 1841, and in particular the Amesbury Woodpecker. Marsh continues "the bird which I have sketched above was killed in the year 1836 in Amesbury Park the residence of Sir E. Antrobus. No other specimen has ever been found in this country. I believe it to be a native of South America. I sent a notice of it to the Editor of this work who did not vouchsafe an answer. The bird is the Golden Winged Woodpecker of South America.* I have never

*Marsh made a very careful and lifelike little coloured picture of the bird and from the illustration in the Audubon Bird Guide and from personal recollections of the Yellow-shafted Flicker in Canada, there is no doubt that the bird was this common species of Woodpecker or Flicker *(Colaptes auratus)* of Eastern North America

R.G.B.

yet heard of any other specimen having been taken in England – it was brought just after it was killed and both my brothers saw it before it was stuffed." Other rarities shot by Marsh included a Honey Buzzard in Draycot Park in 1855 and Rough-legged Buzzard on Somerford Common in 1839.

Of greater interest to us are his notes on common species. "Raven. Two birds rear up their young each year in Draycot Park. Swallow. The improvement in firearms has most unfortunately greatly diminished the numbers of this useful bird. Wanton persons will shoot at them for practice even when they have young. Starling. A very rare bird here until numbers were bought or brought at the expense of Mr. Ferris of the Bell Inn to be shot out of traps, when they escaped and bred in the church tower. Woodcock. In the north of the county where I have often killed it in the summer. Tree Sparrow. Not to be found in this county. Wryneck. Very plentiful at Winterslow. Hooded Crow. Very plentiful in the water-meadows of Salisbury in winter. Common Partridge. Since the introduction of the new Game Laws the number of this common but beautiful bird has very much declined. Dotterel. These birds frequent the Wiltshire Downs in vast flocks in the spring and autumn but they are seldom found in great numbers except for two or three days at each of these seasons, about the time the swallows come and go."

Perhaps unusual among ornithologists were his experiments in edibility and his evident enjoyment of good food. "Redwing. In a mild winter this and the Fieldfare are both good eating. Blackbird. This bird is likewise good eating, especially those which in summer feed on raspberries and other garden plants. Stonechat. This bird with the two next following are very good eating. I have killed hundreds of them for the table on the Winterslow downs. Whinchat, Wheatear. They are well known on our downs where I have killed three or four dozen on a day. Common Bunting. They are good eating in the winter. Yellow Bunting. It is very good eating in the summer. Wood Pigeon. The flesh is delicious when they live on corn but very strong and bad when they are driven in hard weather to eat turnip greens. Capercaillie. They are very good eating and are sold in the market at 5d. a head. They are brought from Norway. Black Grouse. Their flesh is not so good as the Common Grouse. Red-legged Partridge. They are not equal to the Common Partridge in flavour. Quail. Of all game they are the most delicious eating. Golden Plover. The flesh is most delicious, they are plentiful in Salisbury Market in the winter at 1d. a head. Dotterel. They are delicious eating. Lapwing. Their eggs are well known in the London market. Common Curlew. The flesh is almost equal to that of the Woodcock. Common Sandpiper. Their flesh is very good. Landrail. It was very fat and delicious eating. Water Rail. I have killed a great number of these birds, in the water meadows of Salisbury when a boy and found them delicious eating. Moorhen. I have always found them good eating. Coot. The flesh is not so good as the Moorhen. Greylag Goose. I was foolish enough to eat them instead of having them preserved, they were very good eating."

The Rev. Alfred Charles Smith (1822-98) was the son of the Rev. Alfred Smith who had been perpetual curate of Southbroom and later bought and lived at Old Park, Devizes; he was educated at Eton and Christ Church, Oxford, was ordained in 1846 and after marrying in 1851 Frances, daughter of the Rev. T.T. Upwood, in the following year appointed himself Rector of Yatesbury of which he was the Patron. He was a High Churchman and set about the restoration of his church, working with his own hands. He became a Local Secretary of the Wiltshire Archaeological Society on its inauguration in 1853 and in 1857 became one of the General Secretaries which he remained until 1890. For many years he was Editor of the *Wiltshire Archaeological Magazine*. He suffered from his early youth onwards from asthma and bronchitis and for this reason from the age of 17 he went on a series of winter and early spring tours abroad, usually with his father, driving from one country to another. He left four travel books: *The Autobiography of an Old Passport chiefly relating how we accomplished many Driving Tours with our own English Horses, over the Roads of Western Europe, before the time of Railways; Narrative of a Spring Tour in Portugal; The Attractions of the Nile and its Banks. A Journal of Travels in Egypt and Nubia, showing the Attractions to the Archaeologist, the Naturalist and General Tourist;* and *Narrative of a Modern Pilgrimage through Palestine on Horseback and with Tents*. The last was written in the hope of bringing home the facts of Bible history. He visited eleven

European countries and Algeria and over the years he reckoned they had travelled 10,000 miles in their carriages. He writes "Having been obliged to spend many winters and springs in warmer climes . . . I have rambled gun in hand and with binoculars, quite as indispensable a companion to an ornithologist, for several seasons on the southern shores of France and Italy, in Spain and Portugal and above all in Egypt and Nubia and there I have watched in its own home, and studied the habits and life history of many a bird".

He contributed papers on the Ornithology of Wiltshire to the first twelve volumes of the *Magazine* and these he afterwards expanded and published in 1887 as his book *Birds of Wiltshire*. He received a large correspondence from those who had seen, and usually shot, a rare bird and the writer of his obituary describes the gun and skinning knife as his inseparable companions but adds that he always set his face against the extermination of rare species. His own description of his book is "a plain account of the Birds of Wiltshire, written by a Wiltshire man and for Wiltshire people, if I be somewhat old fashioned and behind the times".

His writing is rambling and verbose but he knew his birds and has much to say of their life history and behaviour. To each species he gives the name in French, German, Spanish, Italian and sometimes a Scandinavian language. The book ends with chapters on a Plea for the Rooks and a Plea for Small Birds, directing attention to their usefulness.

There is much that makes melancholy reading today, not only the shooting by collectors but also the commercial slaughter of some species. Of the Skylark he writes "it is killed in astonishing numbers for the table in England, France, Italy and especially Germany. In the London markets alone in 1854, 400,000 are said to have been sold, 25,000 or 30,000 having been often sent together. There can be little doubt that the Skylark must be the most numerous bird, as from a commercial point of view it is one of the most valuable."

A naturalist from childhood, Smith became also an archaeologist and wrote *The Guide to the British and Roman Antiquities of the North Wiltshire Downs* which he published with *The Great Map of a Hundred Square Miles Round Avebury*. This he dedicated to his wife "the constant companion for the last thirty years of my rambles on horseback over the North Wiltshire Downs." He was a member of the British Ornithologists' Union and was in touch with the leading ornithologists including Professor Alfred Newton to whom he dedicated his *Birds of Wiltshire*.

He was a man of great energy. For his church and his other interests he was a tireless worker, always cheerful and much liked. His old enemies asthma and bronchitis caused him to resign from his parish in 1887 and he lived until his death in 1898 in Old Park, Devizes surrounded by his books and his stuffed birds.

The Rev. Arthur P. Morres (1816-1885) was educated at Winchester and became Vicar of Britford. His first published work appears to be on the *Rare Birds of Wiltshire* in the *Zoologist* of 1877. When A.C. Smith ended his articles on the Birds of Wiltshire in the *Wiltshire Archaeological Magazine*, Morres contributed a series on *The Occurrence of some of the Rarer Species of Birds in the Neighbourhood of Salisbury* from 1878 to 1885. He included in this area Christchurch Harbour and the majority of the notes, especially those on sea and water birds, are from outside Wiltshire.

It would seem too, that although he spent some time in the field and also shooting in his younger days these notes were not only the result of his own observations but were largely the contribution of friends and acquaintances, and particularly a number of local bird-stuffers with whom he was in touch. (The term taxidermist was not then in general use.) And what a number there were! Hart of Christchurch of whom he thought most highly, King of Warminster, Harber of Reading, White of Salisbury, Coleman of Marlborough, Lucas of Devizes and Paisley of Swindon. Inevitably there are a great number of anecdotes of how and where birds were shot. But not all ended at a bird-stuffer's. "Imagine my surprise on receiving a kind note from Mr. Henry Blackmore, late of this city, during January 1871, asking me to lunch with him on a certain day, as he thought, being interested in birds, I should like to say that I had partaken of a Salisbury Bustard, for that a female bird had been killed on January 23rd the skin of which had been sent for preservation to King, of Warminster, while the body would be sent up to table on the appointed day. I need not say that I gladly accepted the invitation, and am able to plume myself on having done, what few of my contemporaries have had a chance of doing, i.e. dined off a Salisbury Bustard." This bird was one of a drove of eight which appeared in Devon, four of which were shot before they arrived in Wiltshire, two ended here and the remaining two disappeared.

Sir Everard F. im Thurn, K.C.M.G., K.B.E., C.B., (1852-1912) was educated at Marlborough and Exeter College, Oxford, and also at Edinburgh University; while still at school in 1870 he published a little book on *The Birds of Marlborough* and in 1876 wrote an appendix to it in the *Marlborough College Report*.

In the former he recorded 127 species in the area. Of the Ring Ouzel he wrote "A few specimens visit us every summer, just sufficient to warrant my including it among our regular visitors. It is possible that their eggs have been observed much oftener during the last four years than would appear in the above list. Only those instances have been recorded where the bird itself has been observed to fly off the nest. The nest taken in 1868 was built on the ground at the bottom of a hollow Pollard Willow by the side of the Kennet not far from Ogbourne St. George." The British Trust for Ornithology's *Atlas of Breeding Birds* notes that "up to the end of the 19th Century there were a number of scattered breeding records in lowland England, but such extra-limital nesting has not been reported in this century".

Im Thurn worked for 12 years in British Guiana, first as Curator of Georgetown Museum and then as a special magistrate, when he made several expeditions and greatly increased knowledge of the country's birds. Among those he collected was a new species named after him, *Aegelaus imthurni*. For his services he was made K.C.M.G., and later was Colonial Secretary in Ceylon, Governor of Fiji and High Commissioner for the Western Pacific.

Joshua Reynolds Gascoigne Gwatkin, M.A., M.B.O.U., (1855-1939) was born at Nonsuch House, Bromham and later lived at the Manor House, Potterne. He was a keen sportsman and shot, and a skilled taxidermist, setting up his specimens against appropriate backgrounds. Forty-seven of his cases of birds were presented to the City of Liverpool Museum and five cases to Devizes Museum. He also painted a series of Indian birds while in that country in 1907-8.

George Bathurst Hony (1894-1970) was educated at R.N. College, Osborne and Dartmouth, but was invalided out of the Navy in 1911 when he went up to Cambridge to read Zoology. He served in the 1914-18 war in the 4th Royal Dragoon Guards and in 1920 married Geraldine Birch-Reynardson.

The journal *British Birds* for March 1914 contained his *Notes on the Birds of Wiltshire* which were also reprinted verbatim in the *Wiltshire Archaeological Magazine* June 1915 with the addition of a county bird list. The notes form an appendix to A.C. Smith's *Birds of Wiltshire* and list unsatisfactory records, additional species and rare visitors. He also published a few short notes including one on the spread of the Little Owl and another on the proved breeding of the Curlew near Tidworth. At this time he was only 21 but he writes with authority and had already been elected Member of the British Ornithologists' Union. Observers gave him their field notes but he published few of his own. He presented Devizes Museum with a catalogue of their birds and a copy of his *Notes from the Mediterranean, 1915.*

He published in the *Wiltshire Archaeological Magazine* for 1916 *The Mammals of Wiltshire; Reptiles, Amphibians and Fishes of Wiltshire; Notes on Wiltshire Bats;* and finally *A Bibliography of Wiltshire Zoology*, a list of all papers bearing on the zoology of the county. In this he refers to the vast amount of work done by members of the Marlborough College Natural History Society, especially by E. Meyrick, F.R.S.

After the war Hony farmed in Hampshire and became Agricultural Editor of *The Field*, but ornithology seems to have played no part in his later life.

Lewis Guy Peirson (1897-1957) was born at Exford in Devon, of which his father was Rector. Educated at Oundle and Cambridge, he joined the staff at Marlborough College in 1919, where he taught science until he retired in 1954. He married in 1923 Eveline Clifton who survived him; she shared in all his interests. He was elected a Fellow of the Linnaean Society in 1927.

He served as President of the Marlborough College Natural History Society for 26 years and in 1939 wrote the *Handlist of the Birds of the Marlborough District.* He became the first Chairman of the Natural History Section of the Wiltshire

Archaeological and Natural History Society from the formation of the Section in 1946 until 1951 when he became President of the parent society. He was one of the Recorders of the Wiltshire Bird Notes until 1956. After his retirement he compiled the *Handlist of Wiltshire Birds* published after his death in 1957, a work which involved the checking and analysis of a very large number of records.

His last years were spent in Kingsbridge where the birds of the estuary gave him great pleasure: "I hope there are waders in Heaven". With Guy Peirson we have come from the ornithologists who shot for personal unscientific collections to one who studied birds and flowers with a completely selfless devotion. An old friend described him as a kindly, gentle and most lovable man. His witty writing enchanted the whole family of a fellow recorder fortunate to receive his letters.

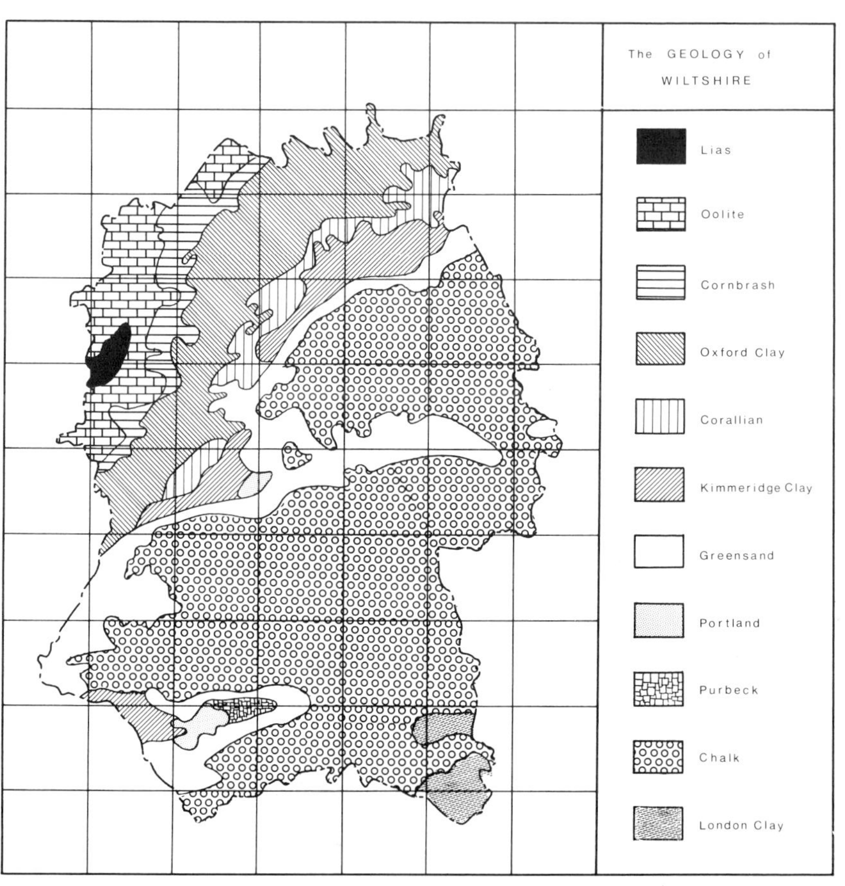
The GEOLOGY of WILTSHIRE
Lias
Oolite
Cornbrash
Oxford Clay
Corallian
Kimmeridge Clay
Greensand
Portland
Purbeck
Chalk
London Clay

THE COUNTY

by Beatrice Gillam

ROUGHLY rectangular in shape, approximately 52 miles (84 km) from north to south and 37 miles (59 km) from east to west, Wiltshire does not fit into any geographical region but lies between the South-West and the South Midlands.

Each side of the rectangle has an affinity with its neighbouring region or county rather than with central Wiltshire located around the town of Devizes. In the north, although the county boundary follows the youthful River Thames for part of its length, the river does not form a natural geographical boundary being almost lost as it flows through the large expanses of water in the gravel pits which straddle the borders of Wiltshire, Gloucestershire and Oxfordshire. In the east the chalk downlands merge into those of Berkshire and Hampshire. In the south, where Salisbury is the focal point, Salisbury Plain creates a natural barrier to the north and the New Forest in Hampshire lies not far away to the south. In the south-west and west Cranborne Chase, the Mendip Hills and Chew Valley Lake are well-known neighbours.

Wiltshire is composed of two main geological strata, the Chalk uplands of the North Wessex Downs, Salisbury Plain and Cranborne Chase and the lowland Oxford and Kimmeridge Clay belts of the north and north-west. Between these, bands of Upper and Lower Greensand separated by Gault clay, are exposed. The Oolitic limestones and clays that form the Cotswold Hills lie along the northern section of the western edge of the county. The massive Chalk outcrops are interrupted by two vales, the Pewsey Vale in the north and the smaller Wardour Vale in the south-west. Both result from the erosion of rocks folded into anticlines along an east-west axis. Tertiary deposits of Bagshot Sand and Reading Clay, which also underlie the New Forest, are exposed in two areas in the south-east corner of the county.

Wiltshire has three river systems. The Thames flowing east across the north of the county is later joined by the Kennet which carries water from the Marlborough Downs. A ridge of

Oxford Clay rising to 400 ft. (122 m.) forms the watershed between the Thames and the Bristol Avon whose catchment area includes the Limestone hills and much of the clay vale of the north and west. From the east, its slow-flowing streams meander in deep channels across the countryside but from the hills in the north-west the By Brook flows swiftly down the steep-sided valleys.

The third and most extensive river system is that of the Salisbury Avon which drains clear water from Salisbury Plain. A small tributary, the Till, flows south to join the east-flowing Wylye which, in turn, is united with the Nadder before joining the Avon at Salisbury. The Bourne, a winterbourne for much of its length, flows into the Avon on the eastern boundary of the city. Finally, the sixth river in the system, the Ebble, flows due east joining the Avon two miles further south on its way through Hampshire to the sea at Christchurch.

Weather records for Wiltshire have been kept at Marlborough College since 1865, at Lackham College of Agriculture since January 1948, at R.A.F. meteorological stations at Boscombe Down since December 1930, Lyneham since November 1942 and Upavon since June 1947. From these sources the mean figures for rainfall, temperature and humidity can be calculated and these show little variation from one part of the county to another. The mean annual temperature is approximately 1°C higher in the west than in the east but there is less than 0.5°C difference between the north and south. Rainfall and humidity are highest in the south-west and lowest in the north-east. In order to place the county's climate in the national context the reader is referred to the map overlays 2 to 5 available for use with *The Atlas of Breeding Birds in Britain and Ireland*. Within this general pattern local variations are apparent particularly in winter when the wind is northerly or easterly. The high, exposed downlands, especially the North Wessex Downs, are then much colder than the lower ground of the Bristol Avon Valley and snow lies above the 700 ft. (215 m.) contour long after it has melted in the rest of the county.

During the years since 1945, which coincide with the period when the bulk of the records in the Systematic List were made, some dramatic extremes of weather were experienced throughout Great Britain. The winters of 1946/7 and 1962/63 and the early months of 1979 were exceptionally cold with heavy falls of snow and long periods when open waters were frozen over and soil temperatures remained below 0°C. During these years the country also suffered the worst drought in recorded history which began in the summer of 1975. There was no prolonged rain that autumn and winter or in the following spring. The summer of 1976 produced the highest temperatures ever recorded and by late June the lack of moisture in the soil (the mean soil temperature at 10 cms. was 20.4°C in July at Lackham) prevented dew formation for many weeks and day-time temperatures regularly exceeded 30°C until the end of August. These conditions resulted in desiccation of the aerial parts of many plants including some shallow rooting tree species, and wildlife in general went through a critical period. The drought was followed by a very wet autumn when Marlborough's September and October mean rainfall of 70.8 mm and 84.4 mm respectively for the previous 112 years was nearly doubled.

POPULATION DISTRIBUTION

Wiltshire is predominantly a rural county, the largest conurbation being at Swindon in the Thames valley. Smaller towns are situated in the Bristol Avon clay vale: Malmesbury, Chippenham, Melksham, Trowbridge and Bradford-on-Avon. The waterless chalkland is sparsely populated, the towns of Westbury, Warminster, Salisbury, Marlborough and Devizes lying on the periphery of approximately 200 square miles (51,800 ha.) of Salisbury Plain. The majority of the villages lie either in the chalk river valleys, along the spring line north of the Plain or above the flood plain of the lowland rivers.

DOWNLAND

(1) The North Wessex Downs run north to south from Swindon to the Pewsey Vale and east to west from the county border to Hackpen Hill and are themselves divided from west to east by the Kennet valley. To the north are the Marlborough Downs, lying mainly between 650-875 feet (200-265 m.) where much of the more gently sloping land is intensively cultivated for cereal crops. In winter, when most of this land has been

either lightly ploughed or winter sown, bare earth becomes the main habitat interrupted by a few hedges, conifer shelter belts and beech hangers. Most of the unploughed downland has been treated with artificial fertiliser and is heavily grazed. Areas of long, semi-natural grassland are mainly confined to track verges and race-horse gallops.

(2) To the south of the River Kennet lies the highest and bleakest ridge of the downland in the county, rising to 964 feet (293 m.) on Milk Hill, with spectacular spurs and steep-sided combes on its south-facing slopes. This is primarily cereal growing country, with a small acreage of kale for winter feed, but the slopes that are too steep to plough remain as permanent pasture grazed by sheep and cattle, 368 acres (148 ha.) of which are unimproved chalk grassland within the Pewsey Downs National Nature Reserve. Knoll Down, north-west of the Devizes/Swindon road near Beckhampton, is a long south-facing slope with long dense grass and developing hawthorn scrub, habitats not found elsewhere in the county except on Salisbury Plain. The chalk ends abruptly at its western end with the steep slopes of Oliver's Castle and Beacon Hill north of Devizes. These are far too steep to plough and there is no grazing. Hedgerows peter out around the 600 foot (182 m.) contour and those on the lower slopes flank the old sheep droves or mark parish boundaries. They are therefore of considerable age and consequently contain many shrub species.

(3) Salisbury Plain with its large tracts of rough grassland which are used as military training areas and dominate the southern half of the county are fully described in another section (page 43).

(4) The chalk uplands south of the Plain are crossed from west to east by the rivers Wylye and Ebble and the Wardour Vale through which the Nadder flows. The most southern hills are the highest, rising to 910 feet (277 m.) at Win Green, and form part of Cranborne Chase. The remainder have no collective name and tend to be regarded as the downs relative to the nearest river. This is the downland of W.H. Hudson, with its steep combes and valleys largely hidden from roads and bleak, open arable land on the tops. There are innumerable old sheep

droves, richly endowed with the best mixed hedgerows in Wiltshire, leading to some of the most species-rich grassland in the county. Small woods, mainly of beech, and areas of mixed scrub which have been retained largely for their sporting value, are scattered throughout these uplands. In 12½ acres (5 ha.) of hawthorn and gorse scrub where a Common Bird Census was carried out for seven years in the 1970's, the average number of breeding species was twenty-five and the total number of pairs (excluding Woodpigeon) 122, or more than ten per acre. Since the temporary decline in the rabbit population following myxomatosis in the 1950's and, in many cases, the change in grazing from sheep to cattle, areas of hawthorn scrub have developed on the steep grass slopes, thus losing grazing acreage but providing an additional wildlife habitat.

OPEN WATER

As in the rest of lowland Britain, all expanses of open water in Wiltshire are man-made. They fall into the following categories: excavated gravel, sand, clay and ironstone pits; lakes in the grounds of large estates where streams flowing from springs below the Greensand have been dammed; a canal and its feeder lake; reservoirs, ponds, watercress beds and, in recent years, pools created for fish farming. Together these represent a wide variety of habitats.

GRAVEL PITS

The largest area of water, the Cotswold Water Park, is fully described in a separate section (page 31).

Gravel has been worked at several sites adjacent to the Bristol Avon between Dauntsey and Chippenham. These provided wetland habitats while being dug and in subsequent years but all have now been filled in and the land reclaimed. The only open water in this valley is at Lacock gravel pit half a mile from the river. In the south gravel is still being won adjacent to the River Wylye at Steeple Langford. Here, a series of worked-out pits are filled with water, one of which is a private Nature Reserve. In the Avon valley south of Salisbury, gravel has also been extracted and the resulting pits at Petersfinger left to develop their natural succession of wetland vegetation which includes stands of *Phragmites*.

SANDPITS

By 1970, all the worked-out sandpits in the county had been filled in or used for tipping but two extensive areas near Calne are still operational and work is planned to continue at one of them until the year 2000. Its after-use is uncertain but it will probably be left as an area of open water. At present there are three small lakes, a reedmace *(Typha latifolia)* bed and a large pit that is being worked dry exposing a vertical face containing a fine white sand.

CLAYPITS

Clay has been dug in north and central Wiltshire and is still being extracted at Purton. Of the disused pits, all those that held water have been filled in except for one north of Devizes.

IRONSTONE PITS

From 1851 to 1901 ironstone was extracted from the Corallian outcrop near Westbury railway station leaving behind a series of deep ponds. Most of the smaller ones have since been filled by controlled tipping but Station, Frogmore and Penleigh Ponds remain, each having a surface area of approximately 6 acres (2.5 ha.). Willow, hawthorn, elder and bramble scrub have developed around them and emergent vegetation includes *Typha.*

LAKES

Of lakes in private estates, Fonthill in the south probably has the best cover and is least disturbed. In the south-west there are lakes at Longleat, Shearwater and Stourhead all of which are open for public recreation of various kinds throughout the year. In the west the estates of the Methuen and Lansdowne families at Corsham and Bowood respectively each have lakes set in landscaped parkland containing mature woodland. Corsham has a large reedbed *(Phragmites communis)* and Bowood has a mixture of deep water and shallow backwaters. In the east, Ramsbury and Chilton Foliat lakes, five miles apart, are 'broadwaters' of the River Kennet.

There are many other privately owned smaller waters throughout the county. For example, at Stanton Fitzwarren, Braydon and Whetham in the north; Erlestoke and The Manor, West Lavington in the centre; and Wincombe, Wardour, Teffont, Compton Chamberlayne and Clarendon in the south.

CANAL

The Kennet and Avon Canal which links the Bristol Avon at Bath with the River Kennet cuts the county in half from west to east. Opened in 1810, the volume of traffic never reached the expectations of the promoters so that the canal steadily declined and became increasingly valuable as a linear wildlife habitat. As maintenance standards slipped, navigation became almost impossible in places by the end of the 1914-18 war and regular traffic ceased in the 1930's. Minimum maintenance has been carried out by the British Waterways Board and there has been restoration work by the Kennet and Avon Canal Trust since the mid-1960's with the aim of opening it throughout its entire length for leisure traffic by the mid-1980's. For about fifty years it remained comparatively undisturbed but, with the expected increase in the amount of motorised craft, its future as a wildlife habitat is likely to be reduced.

CANAL FEEDER LAKES

The main source of water for the canal is Wilton Water near Great Bedwyn. The lake almost dried up during the drought of 1976 and the opportunity was taken to dredge it and subsequently re-landscape the banks. Tockenham Reservoir, near Lyneham, was the feeder lake for the Wiltshire and Berkshire Canal which linked the Bristol Avon with the River Ray, a tributary of the Thames. While the canal no longer has any open water, except for a short stretch in Swindon, the reservoir remains.

RESERVOIR

Coate Water, a reservoir on the edge of Swindon to part of which the public has access, was enlarged to 114 acres (45.8 ha.) in 1974 by the excavation of a new lake on its eastern side and the latter was designated as Wiltshire's first Local Nature Reserve. The two lakes have a variety of water depths and the new one has provided marsh and island habitats additional to the well developed *Phragmites* beds and scrub which fringe the old lake. Swindon also has two small amenity lakes, Liden Lagoon and Shaftesbury Avenue Lakes which assist in flood prevention and are developing into good wildlife areas.

PONDS

Although most farm and village ponds no longer serve their original purposes, and indeed many have been filled in, those that do survive are less disturbed than when in use and have become miniature wildlife sanctuaries. The 'Save the Village Pond' campaign, initiated by the Ford Motor Company in 1974, combined with work carried out by the Wiltshire Wildlife Conservation Corps and the British Trust for Conservation Volunteers, have made a contribution to pond restoration including that of two dewponds.

WATERCRESS/FISH FARMING

The pure water of the chalk rivers and streams is ideal for growing watercress and until the 1970's this was a profitable business. In recent years the number of cress beds has diminished, several having been converted to the more lucrative trade of fish farming.

RIVERS

(1) The Bristol Avon flows mainly through open pastureland but its water becomes relatively more polluted as it passes through the industrial towns of Malmesbury, Chippenham, Melksham and Bradford-on-Avon. It is described in detail in a separate section (page 37).

(2) The Salisbury Avon, its tributaries and the River Kennet all rise in the chalk. The calcium-rich water is free of industrial pollution enabling submerged plants such as Water Crowfoot to flourish and provide the right conditions for an abundance of insect nymphs and larvae which emerge at the height of the bird breeding season. There is a variety of habitats, in addition to the aquatic ones, associated with these rivers as they meander through narrow valleys not exceeding half-a-mile (0.8 km) in width for much of their length. There is a mosaic of villages and

meadows, some of the smaller ones being old water-meadows that have not been drained. In the Avon valley at Woodford and Britford are water-meadows that are still worked in the traditional manner. The thick hedgerows with willow and ash trees are a feature of the Bourne valley. All the rivers have many road and foot bridges while weirs and fords remain in some places.

SEWAGE FARMS

From the ornithological point of view the most important sewage farm in the county has always been the one provided for Swindon, the largest town, which had a population of about 60,000 in 1940. Up to that time it was the old-fashioned, open type with a variety of wetland habitats. Modernisation began after the second world war leaving a sludge area but today the sewage farm is very modern with few remaining wetland habitats. South Cerney sewage farm lies just outside Wiltshire's northern boundary on the edge of the Cotswold Water Park. Here too, modern treatment works are nearing completion and soon this habitat will be lost leaving old type sewage farms only near the smaller towns.

RUBBISH TIPS

The use of rubbish tips for the disposal of solid waste may also soon become a thing of the past as available holes in the ground are filled and the land reclaimed. Pensworth tip near Salisbury is probably the largest, with other tips being scattered throughout the county to serve the smaller towns. These include one in the worked-out part of the Calne sand pits and, in recent years, a hole was dug on the Larkhill Ranges for use by the public. Swindon now incinerates its waste and a cement factory near Westbury uses rubbish to fuel its fires.

AIRFIELDS

Airfields in Wiltshire, some of which are not now regularly used by aircraft, occupy over 4,000 acres (1,600 ha.). These large areas of open grass which is kept short by mowing during its growing season, together with the hardstandings and old tracks, contribute additional habitats. They are well distributed over the county. Those at Upavon, Netheravon and Boscombe

Down all lie on the downland escarpment east of the Salisbury Avon, while those at Lyneham and Hullavington are either side of the Bristol Avon and Colerne is on the extreme tip of the southern spur of the Cotswolds. In the north, there is a large airfield at Wroughton; at Keevil near Trowbridge there is a disused one used irregularly for parachuted load drops and there is another totally disused one at Zeals in the south-west.

PEWSEY VALE

The Pewsey Vale lies west to east across the middle of Wiltshire between the North Wessex Downs and Salisbury Plain and is therefore relatively sheltered. It varies in width from four miles (6½ km.) in the west to two and a half miles (4 km.) in the east at an altitude not varying much from the 400 foot (122 m.) contour. It has no river flowing through it but the tributary streams of the Salisbury Avon, all of which rise at the foot of the downs on the north, cut their way through it in deep twisting channels before they flow into the main river near Upavon. Adjacent to these streams, especially in the Pewsey/Woodborough section, are small marshy areas. Most of these are unmanaged and have developed either into woodland dominated by alder and willow with a ground flora of sedge, iris, meadowsweet etc. or in stands of coarse sedges, which include tussock sedge *(Carex paniculata)* as at Jones's Mill Nature Reserve or into stands of *Phragmites* as at Sharcott. Most of the drier land has been drained and cultivated. Until the 1970's, one of the most striking features of the vale were the hedgerow elm trees which, by the end of that decade had all but vanished through Dutch elm disease.

SOUTH-EAST WILTSHIRE

The south-east of Wiltshire, lying roughly south of the Salisbury/Romsey road is unlike any other part of the county and is really part of the New Forest. The heavy damp soils support fine old oak woodlands with an understorey of hazel which is still coppiced in a few places for hurdle making. There are also large areas of open heathland with scattered birch, Scots pine and hawthorn.

WOODLANDS

by David Rice

THE distribution of the major woodlands had been established by 1086 and the production of Domesday Book. It has been calculated that the total woodland was 149,398 acres (60,502 ha.) representing 17.4% of the county's area, contained in the Forests of Braydon, Chute, Claydon, Grovely, Melksham, Pewsham, Savernake, Tilshead, and parts of Kemble, Selwood and Cranborne Chase. With the exception of Kemble and Tilshead, remnants of all these forests exist today.

The most recent estimate for woodland, 1957, is 57,000 acres (23,000 ha.), representing 6.6% of the county's area, of which 6,000 acres (2,400 ha.) were beechwood. The area of coniferous and mixed high forest in 1948 was 8,000 acres (3,200 ha.).

The Forestry Commission manages some 11,800 acres (4,800 ha.) and 22,000 acres (8,900 ha.) are privately owned and subject to the Forestry Commission Dedicated Woodland Scheme, though not all are actively managed. The balance of 23,000 acres (9,300 ha.) is mainly small woods, copses and shelter belts, generally lacking formal management.

In the last 22 years changes have taken place, but these have not been quantified accurately. Woodland has been felled and the land converted to agriculture; currently at the rate of approximately 40 acres (16 ha.) per annum. Conversely, afforestation has been undertaken, particularly by the Ministry of Defence, on Salisbury Plain for military training purposes and by some landowners, for purposes of sport. Frequently, native broad-leaved shrubs are incorporated, thus providing good song-bird habitats.

It is unlikely that, in the foreseeable future, any major forest additions will occur, as these would have to be at the expense of agricultural land that is vastly more profitable in its present use. Significant losses are unlikely to occur in the larger woodlands, most of which are owned by, or on a long lease to, the Forestry Commission, or are managed under a Forestry Commission Dedication Scheme. Some measure of control is exercised over the balance of smaller woods and copses through the Forestry

Commission Felling Licence Regulations and the Commission's consultation with the Local Authority. Those areas that are outside the above provisions, e.g. scrub hawthorn on downland, are at risk.

The main Forestry Commission holdings are the remnants of Braydon Forest, near Purton, on the Oxford Clay; Spye Park near Chippenham, on the Lower Greensand; Savernake Forest and West Woods near Marlborough; the remnants of Chute Forest near Collingbourne Ducis; the outliers of Cranborne Chase at Stonedown and Vernditch, near Broadchalke; the remnants of Clarendon Forest, east of Salisbury, and part of Grovely Forest, west of Salisbury, mainly on Clay with Flint, overlying Upper and Middle Chalk. The major private woodlands are confined to the Greensand at Longleat, Maiden Bradley and Stourhead in Selwood Forest, to similar soils at Fonthill and the Vale of Wardour, west of Tisbury, to the Tertiary Sands near Redlynch, south-east of Salisbury and to Clay with Flint at Grovely and Great Ridge, west of Salisbury, and Cranborne Chase, near Tollard Royal.

As these major woodlands are managed to produce maximum yields, conifers are the main species planted. When broadleaves are planted, in mixture with conifers, they are found more often in the private woodlands. These newly planted areas, no matter what species are used, provide suitable nesting habitats for Grasshopper Warblers for some seven years. This situation is more likely to prevail in woodlands on the Greensand and Tertiary sands that are most suited to conifers, but it may be partially reversed on other soil types where enhanced grant aid from the State leads to the establishment of, generally native, broadleaved species. Crossbills feed in the conifer plantations in most years; indeed breeding is suspected at Maiden Bradley. Bramblings frequent the older beechwoods during the winter.

Woodlands, which form a significant portion, or the entirety of, each of twenty Nature Conservancy Council designated Sites of Special Scientific Interest, are Oak, Oak/Ash or Beech dominated. They have been primarily designated by virtue of their botanical or entomological interest; ornithological interest is mentioned for only three sites. These are Hamptworth Common, Savernake Forest and Spye Park. Hamptworth Common is an area of acid heath and bog, typical of the New

Forest of which it is geographically a part and thus unique in Wiltshire. The common is dominated by Scots Pine, with a few areas of Birch. Savernake Forest, a relic of a medieval Royal Forest, has groups of Sessile Oak and areas of Beech with a number of areas of sparse scrub along shallow valleys that bisect the forest, where Redstarts may be seen. The broadleaved areas, mainly adjacent to the major rides, are to be retained and the balance will continue as a commercially productive woodland. Spye Park is a very diverse habitat of heath, scrub parkland, woodland marsh and alder carr; the last is of particular significance for Siskin and Redpoll.

Mention must be made of the "Wiltshire Weed", the elm tree. Though rarely a woodland tree it was the dominant or co-dominant tree species over some 60% of the county, particularly on the non-chalk soils. Richard Jefferies, in 1879, described the vales as appearing to consist of one vast forest instead of the innumerable meadows which were really there, and, over a century earlier, William Marshall said: "the eye seems ever on the verge of a forest, which is, as it were by enchantment, continually changing into inclosures and hedgerows".

In 1972 the total Wiltshire elm population was estimated to be 1,000,000; it is now almost nil as a result of the ravages of the aggressive strain of the Dutch Elm disease. It is possible that some of the suckers will survive and grow into trees, but the likelihood of a return to the former level of tree cover seems remote.

The elm disaster has spurred landowners and farmers into considering tree planting. The level of planting, with the help of professional advice and financial assistance from the State, of mainly broadleaved species in sites compatible with modern agricultural practice is increasing.

Undoubtedly this great loss of elms will have affected some bird species, which will have lost nesting sites. As elm is comparatively poor in the range of insects living on it, 80 species, compared with 284 on oak, this loss of food sources is less important. Rooks are perhaps the greatest sufferers, though there was a national pre-Dutch Elm disease decline, of 43% since 1946, and a further survey is required to evaluate the post-Dutch Elm disease population. In the 1975 survey the tree species were identified for some 70% of the nests recorded, and

47% of these were elm. Subsequently, Rooks have been recorded nesting on electricity pylons and also, more frequently, in trees of lesser stature than those used in the past. These signs of adapted behaviour of the bird species mentioned above give hope for their healthy survival.

Summary

The woodlands of Wiltshire are varied in structure, dominated by conifers on the Greensand and broadleaves on the other soil types. Their boundaries are unlikely to change but their broadleaved content is likely to increase. The elms have all gone and many small copses too, but trees are being planted, at an increasing rate, in the open countryside.

COTSWOLD WATER PARK

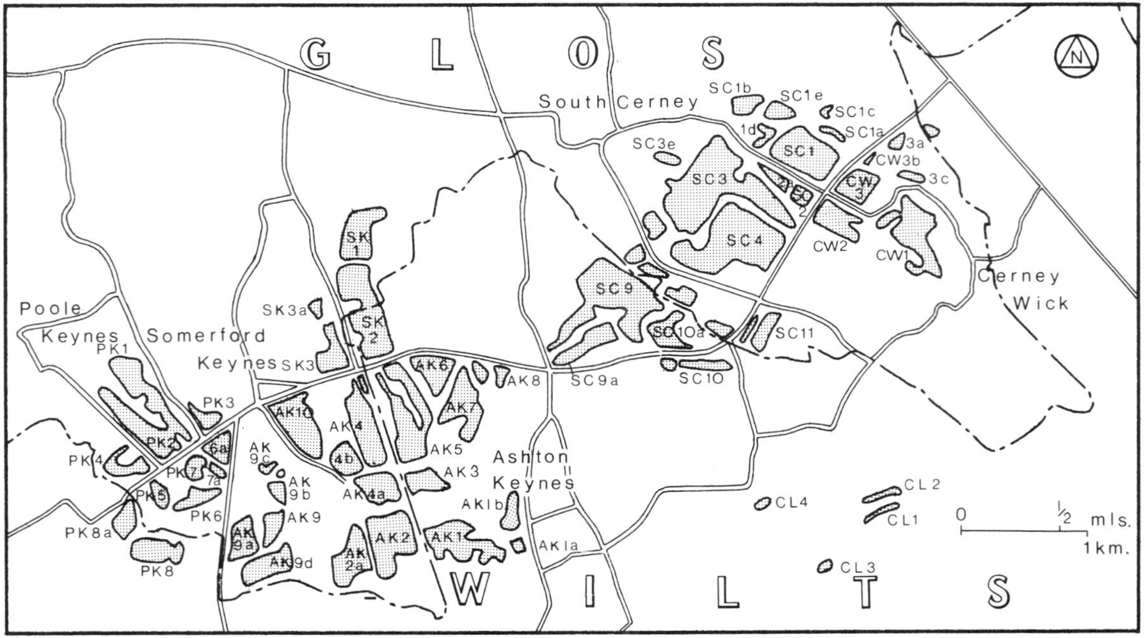

THE COTSWOLD WATER PARK

by Geoffrey Snowball

THE Cotswold Water Park, situated in the Upper Thames valley, contains the largest concentration of gravel pits in the country. Gravel has been extracted from the area since the 1920's resulting in the creation of a series of closely associated lakes and a wetland area of national importance. Two separate sections form the Cotswold Water Park. An eastern section lies wholly in Gloucestershire between Fairford and Lechlade, and a larger western section is sited on the Gloucestershire/Wiltshire border between Cirencester and Cricklade. The respective total water areas are about 577 acres (231 ha.) and 845 acres (338 ha.) within a combined land area of about 14,250 acres (5,700 ha.). Future planned gravel extraction from the surrounding agricultural landscape will considerably increase the water areas. Many of the lakes have been given over to recreational uses such as fishing, sailing and water-skiing. Birds that are disturbed by these activities are able to find refuge on quieter pits. The oolitic limestone gravel beds are saturated with water and lie on an impervious layer of Oxford clay. During the excavation of gravel the pits are kept generally free of water by pumping. Shallow pools are left with lengths of irregular water edges. Once extraction ceases however, the pits rapidly fill with calcium-rich water resulting in the formation of marl lakes. Many species of aquatic vegetation rapidly become established which support a rich animal life. With the rough ground surrounding the pits quickly becoming coarsely vegetated, an environment is produced that is attractive to the resident birds, the breeding visitors and the migrants. A total of 187 species has been recorded in the Cotswold Water Park.

The Cotswold Water Park (West) has 66 gravel pits of which 19½ are in Wiltshire near the village of Ashton Keynes. One pit is bisected by the counties' border. They range in size from approximately 2½ acres (1 ha.) to 62 acres (25 ha.) and form the most important area of standing water in the county. The following is an account of the species that have been recorded in the Wiltshire area. As birds have no respect for man-made boundaries many species occur with greater regularity and in larger numbers when the whole of the western section is considered. Some species have occurred in one county's area and not in the other area. For example a Little Auk in 1975 and a Hen Harrier and an Alpine Swift in 1977 were recorded in Gloucestershire. A Wood Warbler was seen in 1977 and 1979 in Wiltshire, and the only Black-throated Diver, in 1972, before the remarkable influx into the country in February 1979 when at least four birds of the latter species occurred on several pits in the western section. Sometimes both counties can claim a significant record, as happened in 1975 when a Buff-breasted Sandpiper first seen in Wiltshire flew off over Gloucestershire, and in 1977 when a Pectoral Sandpiper divided its time in the area between the two counties. These are the only nearctic waders to have occurred in the Cotswold Water Park, both in the autumn. In the case of a Gannet in 1977, which was eventually shot, the bird must have flown over Wiltshire as it traversed almost the length of the western section between its fishing pits, but was only recorded in Gloucestershire.

The many different types of habitat provide breeding areas for a variety of birds. Most pits have sufficient emergent vegetation to accommodate a pair of Great Crested Grebes with the pairs of Coots. One or two pairs of Little Grebes inhabit the shallower pits. Recently a pair of Greylag Geese and Red-crested Pochards have nested. A small feral population of Greylag Geese appears to be establishing itself in the Cotswold Water Park (West), and a pair or two of Red-crested Pochards, no doubt of escape origins, have been resident for a number of years. During the winter the latter species increases slightly, mainly with the addition of male birds. Other nesting water birds include Mute Swan, an occasional pair of Canada Geese, and where the vegetation is dense round the edges of pits, Mallard and Tufted Duck.

There is ample opportunity for the Cuckoo to select a host species. Small reed and osier beds which develop on the mature pits hold Reed Warbler and Reed Bunting. Species which occupy the hedgerows and areas of bushes and brambles include Turtle Dove, Sedge Warbler, Whitethroat, Lesser Whitethroat, Greenfinch, Bullfinch and Linnet. Sometimes the Nightingale will nest in the denser parts. In the more open grassy areas

Skylarks and some Yellow Wagtails are found. Where the ground is marshy one or two pairs of Redshanks breed. Sometimes during daylight the Little Owl can be seen hunting.

A small copse contains the only heronry in the Cotswold Water Park. It was estabished in 1968 and numbers of nests have varied up to a maximum of 21 in 1975. Birds breeding in and around the small deciduous wood, which is bisected by the River Isis (Thames), include Willow Warbler, Chiffchaff, Blackcap, Treecreeper, Spotted Flycatcher, Tree Sparrow, Great Spotted Woodpecker and a pair or two of Jays. With the exception of the Willow Tit, where breeding has to be confirmed, the rest of the tit family and the Long-tailed Tit are resident. Breeding has also to be confirmed for the Green Woodpecker.

Two species whose breeding presence is entirely dependent on the extraction of gravel are the Sand Martin and the Little Ringed Plover. Where a sheer side to a pit is formed the Sand Martin usually establishes a colony. Approximately 220 holes have been counted in one large colony. Generally every year there is enough exposed gravel in one or two pits to accommodate up to four pairs of Little Ringed Plovers. Their success rate of rearing young is not high due to the hazards they face of the nest site being flooded if pumping ceases, and corvid predation.

During winter the near-deserted waters of summer, by comparison, are alive with water birds. Numbers are variable as there is a considerable movement within the Cotswold Water Park (West), and much greater numbers are counted in the Gloucestershire area. In the Wiltshire area Pochard numbers have been in excess of 800, Tufted Duck about 400, Teal up to 100 and Coot about 1000. There is an increase in the population of Mute Swan, Great Crested Grebe and, in particular, Mallard. It is not unusual to see about 30 Great Crested Grebes on a pit if there is disturbance on some of the other pits. Wigeon and Goldeneye tend to favour pits in the Gloucestershire area and so numbers are small. Sometimes however flocks of up to 200 Wigeon overfly the Wiltshire area.

Large flocks of Lapwings congregate on the surrounding farmland, the build-up usually starting in July, and can number about 4,000. Up to 600 Golden Plovers often associate with the Lapwings. The presence of some Golden Plovers of the northern race becomes apparent during the acquisition of breeding plumage prior to their departure to the breeding grounds. Small flocks of Redwings and Fieldfares and mixed flocks of finches, which at times include a few Redpolls, move around the area. Gulls, with the exception of the Great Black-backed Gull which rarely occurs, are well represented. There is a gull roost in the Gloucestershire part which has contained up to 7,000 Black-headed Gulls, several hundred Common Gulls and up to 700 Lesser Black-backed Gulls. Herring Gulls are considerably fewer. Some regular winter visitors are Cormorant, Gadwall, Shoveler, Shelduck and Water Rail. Rare visitors have included Red-throated and Great Northern Divers, Whooper and Bewick's Swans, Pintail, Ruddy Duck, Long-tailed Duck, Smew, Peregrine and Jack Snipe.

During the spring and autumn passages, March to June and July to October, there is a regular movement of many species, and often the unusual is recorded. One or two birds of the race of Pied Wagtail *Motacilla a. alba* and of both races of Rock Pipit are sometimes identified in spring. A feature in recent years has been the appearance of Hobbies seen hawking for insects, with the occasional sighting in summer when hunting among the hirundines and swifts. Common species occurring include Meadow Pipit, Wheatear, Stonechat and a few Whinchats. Rarities have been a Spoonbill in 1978, two Ospreys in 1976 and a few Little Gulls. In the small tern passage the most frequent visitor is the Common Tern. In 1979 a pair nested for the first time in the county and the Water Park, successfully rearing three young. They again nested successfully in 1980. The Arctic Tern is a rare visitor, and since the birds can be well seen few remain unidentified. Black Terns are quite scarce, normally appearing in the autumn. A flock of 20 in August 1978 was part of an exceptional passage of at least 67 Black Terns in the Cotswold Water Park over a two-day period. Three Little Terns in September 1975 were the seventh county record for this species.

The majority of the county's wader records come from its area in the Cotswold Water Park (West) which lies on the migration route from the Wash to the Severn Estuary. Generally numbers are in ones and twos with greater frequency during the autumn passage. Dunlin and Ringed Plover are quite regular, often occurring together, Ruff are fairly regular and Curlew are often seen in small numbers. The Greenshank appears to be increasing with up to eight birds seen throughout the autumn. The species moves about quite freely between the pits in the counties, and can total double figures in the western section.

The commonest waders are the Green Sandpiper, which is absent only during May and the first half of June, and the Common Sandpiper. They rarely reach double figures at any one time, even though maximum autumn counts in the western section have been 45 Green Sandpipers and 29 Common Sandpipers. A reason for this is that most 'dry pits', which the Green Sandpiper prefers, and most mature pits, the gravelly margins of which the Common Sandpiper prefers, develop in Gloucestershire.

Occasionally a species has occurred in exceptional numbers. There was a remarkable influx of the very rare Little Stint in September 1976 when up to eight birds were present throughout the month in one pit. Water levels were lowered by the drought of that year exposing large areas of mud. This, and a good breeding season coupled with the favourable weather while the birds were on passage may have been factors influencing this notable occurrence. Other flocks have been 22 Greenshanks in autumn 1975, 17 Ruffs and 12 of the rare Black-tailed Godwit in the springs of 1976 and 1979 respectively.

Waders that have rarely occurred are Oystercatchers, Grey Plover, Turnstone, for which five of the county's seven records, all in recent years, have been on the Water Park, Whimbrel, which have occurred in a flock of five, Wood Sandpiper and Sanderling. In May 1977 a Kentish Plover was recorded for the first time in the county. Although originally seen in Gloucestershire it flew into Wiltshire. This was the second record for this species in the Cotswold Water Park, and while present in Gloucestershire there were Ringed and Little Ringed Plover at the same pit, providing a unique opportunity to compare the three species. The same year produced two further birds, both in Gloucestershire.

In recent years there has been a considerable increase in the activities of local birdwatchers on the Cotswold Water Park. Most birdwatching is conducted at weekends and it is interesting to conjecture, in the light of some of the occurrences, what is not observed during the week. A reasonable conclusion would be, that as birds do not confine their movements to weekends, much is missed. Some birds remain only for a brief period before they elect to move on, or are persuaded to do so by the activities of gravel extraction.

Most pits on the Cotswold Water Park are private property and permission is required to enter. Many however are adjacent to roads and the few public footpaths and this allows the visitor ample opportunity to explore the area. Species are continually being added to the checklist and will continue to be added as the area expands.

THE BRISTOL AVON

by John Buxton and John Govett

IN contrast to the chalk uplands which cover most of the rest of the county the Clay Vale of the Bristol Avon is characterised by numerous villages scattered fairly evenly over the landscape, but its rurality has in recent years been much diminished by the intrusion of electricity pylons and other constructions. The Vale contains six of the ten largest towns in Wiltshire with a population of c. 155,000 in 1971.

In ancient times this region was almost completely forested, with the oak *(Quercus robur)* as the dominant species. There were marshy tracts in several areas, where surviving placenames indicate their existence. In historical times man has drastically altered the landscape by felling and draining, with the result that most of the land is now rich pasture for dairy cattle, interspersed with woods and copses of deciduous trees, with larger areas of woodland in the northern part of the vale; but Picket Wood, near Trowbridge, has been partially replanted with conifers. More recently the familiar English countryside pattern of fields surrounded by hedgerows has emerged, but modern mechanization has resulted in the loss of many stretches of hedgerow, in which hawthorn predominates. This has had an adverse effect on such species as the Dunnock and Greenfinch, which rely on hedges for nest sites. In many places hedges are trimmed very thoroughly by machine, and all scrubby, overgrown patches are eliminated. This has resulted in a very 'overgardened' countryside which lacks diversity of vegetation, and where such species as Nightingale, Whitethroat and Garden Warbler suffer. Elms had been extensively planted as hedgerow trees, but the great majority are now dead or dying as a result of Dutch Elm disease: the resultant landscapes resemble a Flanders battlefield in 1918. For a few years woodpeckers will have a plentiful supply of insect food, but as the dead trees are removed their population will no doubt decline once more. Where replanting is taking place other species such as lime (*Tilia* spp.) or oak (*Quercus* spp.) are used. The clays retain moisture and the beech *(Fagus sylvatica)* does not thrive, and many were lost in the drought of

1976. Bramblings and other birds which like beech-mast are therefore not numerous.

The major part of the region, lying on the Oxford Clay, is mostly undulating, but the flood plain of the river is very flat and near Chippenham flooding is frequent. The upper reaches of the river, north of Chippenham, have considerable stretches of deciduous woodland. There is, perhaps, a larger variety of species here than lower down and in twenty-five years one of us (J.B.) recorded one hundred and six species in or near a garden which was c. 500 yards (450 m.) from the Avon. A few of these were casuals, such as Pied Flycatcher, Peregrine and White-fronted Goose, and also a Red-headed Bunting which appeared in two not consecutive years, but was no doubt an 'escape'. His own small collection of duck probably attracted Wigeon, Gadwall, Pintail and Shoveler, but Teal and Pochard (which were never kept) also came to his acre of water on occasion. There remain eighty-five or ninety species which may be regarded as regular. The Avon's one fast-flowing tributary, the By Brook in the north-west of the county, is the haunt of Dippers, found nowhere else on the river.

Kingfishers are numerous, returning year after year to the same nesting sites in the banks, in spite of sometimes losing their broods through flooding. One year seventeen were ringed in one garden, to which they came up in late summer; in winter they occasionally enter urban areas, and one has been seen flying over Trowbridge, rising to clear the roofs. Sand Martins do not nest in the river banks above Chippenham, but some are present lower down. A few pairs of Mute Swans nest every year, and more than a few Little Grebes, Mallard and Moorhens in the riverside vegetation; some farmers encourage the Mallard to nest, to provide sport in winter. There are two heronries, at Great Bradford Wood and Bowood, and odd pairs breed from time to time away from the main colonies. Reed Buntings are present, but only here and there; but Grey Wagtails are numerous, even in Malmesbury town, and they also nest by still water away from the river. Common Sandpipers appear every spring on their passage north, and Green Sandpipers are present each winter. Snipe are seldom seen in the upper reaches, and then only singly, but below Chippenham quite large parties may be found in wet patches. A few pairs of Redshank and Curlew nest in most years. Big flocks of Lapwing, two thousand or more in a flock, come in autumn and remain until hard weather drives them further west, but only a few pairs remain to breed. Ringed Plovers have been seen running about wet runways at Keevil airfield, as if they were on a beach. Occasionally a pair or two of Woodcock nest in the area, but they are not numerous even in autumn.

In the pastures and leys there used to be numbers of Yellow Wagtails until the drought in the Sahel caused huge losses to the wintering birds about 1969, as also to Whitethroats and Spotted Flycatchers. Pied Wagtails remain common everywhere, though perhaps not very much outnumbering the Greys; but they have adapted more thoroughly to man-made habitats, such as filter-beds at sewage works, and they roost in trees or on buildings in several of the towns. Skylarks and Meadow Pipits are rather scarce, only becoming more conspicuous as one approaches the downs.

In autumn and winter great flocks of Common Gulls flight in from their roost on the Severn near Berkeley; up to two thousand may be counted in a single field when ploughing is in progress in the upper reaches of the river. Lower down Black-headed Gulls seem to be much more numerous, probably coming from the roost on Chew Valley Lake. A few Lesser Black-backed Gulls, and an occasional Herring Gull, may be seen in autumn and winter. Common and Arctic Terns are sometimes seen flying along the river on migration and one of us (J.G.) once watched a Common Tern feeding on shoaling Bleak *(Alburnus alburnus)* near Staverton.

About the farms and villages Swallows and House Martins abound; even in Malmesbury itself there is a flourishing colony of House Martins, with nests in the High Street, in the Market Square and in Abbey Row. Swifts too, as dependent as the hirundines on man-made nesting sites, are to be found throughout the area where old buildings provide suitable nest-sites. "Malmesbury Jackdaws" have long been notorious, and there are large flocks in winter; they may originally have provided a nick-name for the Benedictine monks at the Abbey, whose black and grey habit resembles theirs. Rooks are plentiful, though Dutch Elm disease has deprived them of many traditional nesting sites; here and there they have taken to nesting on electricity pylons.

Carrion Crows, Magpies and Jays have all benefited from the decline in keepering, to the detriment of small hedgerow birds, and parties of Jays, ten or more together, gather at oak trees to feed on acorns. Sparrowhawks have also increased recently, and have been seen to take young Magpies. Of the other predators, Kestrels are common and there have been recent breeding records of Buzzard and Hobby. Barn Owl, Tawny Owl and Little Owl are all present, but the Barn Owl has decreased over the last twenty-five years, and so, perhaps, has the Little Owl.

As usual in lowland England the great majority of species were originally woodland birds which often now have to make do with hedgerows (a diminishing habitat) and with parks and gardens. All the tits except the Crested Tit are here, Treecreeper, Wren and Nuthatch, though the last has never recovered since the disastrous winter of 1962-63. Seven species of warbler breed and Nightingales can be found in most likely-looking woods. Pigeons are all too abundant – the Collared Dove began to breed here in 1967 – and only the Turtle Dove is rather scarce. Of the thrushes Blackbird, Song Thrush and Mistle Thrush are all numerous, and there are usually large flocks of Fieldfares and Redwings in winter. Robins abound, and a few pairs of Redstarts nest on the border with Gloucestershire where, in one recent year, there was also a pair of Stonechats. Wheatears are seen quite frequently on passage, but are not likely to breed. Of the finches, Chaffinch, Greenfinch, Goldfinch and Bullfinch are common everywhere; Linnets, rather surprisingly, much less so. Hawfinches are present but, as always, very elusive, and though Bramblings, Siskins and Redpolls come in winter there never seem to be many of these. Of the buntings, only the Yellowhammer and the Reed Bunting seem to be present, and these in small numbers. Tree Sparrows are plentiful in some years and apparently absent in others. The three woodpeckers all breed here.

Braydon Pond, the one large stretch of open water, is much less rewarding than it was twenty years ago, perhaps because of its exploitation as a trout hatchery, or perhaps because of the great increase in the area of water in the Cotswold Water Park. Whatever the reason, Wigeon and Shoveler seldom now appear, and there are fewer Pochard and Tufted Duck than there were. Coot are common enough, but one does not see them there in hundreds any more. Great Crested and Little Grebes breed in undiminished numbers, and there are occasional visits from a Red-throated Diver, a Cormorant or a Goosander. One or two pairs of Herons have nested here and there in the area, but there is no well-established heronry and most of the herons that visit probably come in from Bowood.

SALISBURY PLAIN

by Geoffrey Boyle

SALISBURY Plain is an undulating plateau with deep gullies covered by Upper Chalk, with the exception of the Wylye Valley and the Northern part where Melbourn Rock plays an important part. It is roughly 26 miles (41.8 km.) from East to West and 20 miles (32.2 km.) from North to South – a total area of 320,000 acres (128,000 ha.). It has a clear-cut boundary on the North and West sides as a result of steep escarpments overlooking the Vale of Pewsey and the country beyond Warminster. On the South side it is considered to finish at the Vale of Wardour and to the East at the valley of the Salisbury Avon. The bottoms of the valleys average about 250 feet (75 m.) above sea level and the high ground rises to 350/400 feet (105/120 m.) with the high points such as Westbury Hill reaching 755 feet (230 m.).

The perimeter is largely cultivated and put down to crops of wheat and barley, while sheep and cattle graze the remaining grassland. Two-thirds of the plain is "out of bounds" to the public; since the First World War an area of some 90,000 acres (36,000 ha.), or a quarter of the whole, has been used as artillery ranges and military training areas. This has resulted in valuable conservation of the natural chalk grassland, which for years was short cropped by vast flocks of sheep and by rabbits before the onslaught of myxomatosis.

The Plain has some beautiful valleys through which runs a series of rivers all draining towards Salisbury, the main ones being the Avon, the Wylye, the Nadder and the Ebble. This makes for a wide variety of habitat supporting both aquatic and downland birds. In addition to the rivers there are bournes which in the summer are mostly dry, but in the winter and spring fill up and result in areas of wet land where waders such as Snipe and Redshank occur and possibly breed; Black-tailed Godwits have also been seen on rare occasions. This account refers only to the chalk uplands.

In the past conifers and beeches were planted by landowners as cover for Pheasants and in these plantations brambles offer good feeding areas for Wrens, and for Whitethroats and other summer migrants; Nightingales may be heard singing in day-time from some thickets. Blackthorn, Elder, Gorse, and to a lesser extent Juniper, are dotted over the plain and these vantage points are much favoured by Stonechats and Whinchats. The banks along the roadsides make ideal nesting sites for the Stonechat, while gentle grassy slopes afford equally good breeding territory for Whinchats.

Salisbury Plain provides a vast natural domain for raptors: Hen Harriers can be seen frequently in winter lazily floating over the ranges and with luck a Montagu's Harrier will pass through in the spring. Little was known of the roosting habits on the Plain by Hen Harriers until December 1977 when two males and two females were seen to drop into long grass to roost at dusk. From January 1978 onwards the roost was under regular observation – males usually outnumbering females – and on the 4th April 1978 five males flew in. A single female was present from 18th to the 23rd April and after this date no further birds were seen. In February 1979 two males and three females roosted in a different locality.

Hobbies breed regularly, but numbers seem to be falling as disturbance increases. Merlins, though never common, are recorded every winter and both sexes have been seen which indicates the possibility of breeding having occurred during the summer although there is no definite proof. The Buzzard bred regularly until the mid-fifties when the onslaught of myxomatosis decimated the rabbit population, thereby reducing severely the staple diet of the Buzzard, and this seriously affected the number of breeding pairs. They are now recovering and may be seen at times in most parts of the Plain. Rough-legged Buzzards put in an appearance on rare occasions in winter and in a good year more than one bird may be recorded. Such a winter was 1974/75 when a large influx took place in Britain which spilled over into Wiltshire.

Short-eared Owls may be seen hunting along the ridges in daylight during most winters and occasionally they stay until the late spring. In 1964 a pair raised young, in spite of nesting in the middle of an impact area on one of the artillery ranges. Numbers appear to be governed by the supply of short-tailed field voles and in a bad vole year no Short-eared Owls are recorded. In recent years it has been noticed that Kestrels are piratical on Short-eared Owls and there is documented evidence of a Kestrel actually taking prey away from one of them. The Little Owl used to be common and in 1951 for example, the "vermin" bag for a game shoot on the ranges included 17: now only a few pairs breed each year in spite of protection.

Mention of Salisbury Plain usually conjours up in one's mind two particular species, the Great Bustard and the Stone Curlew. The former was already uncommon in the 16th century and afterwards became gradually scarcer. They were rare by 1800 and the last record of breeding is in 1806. Since that date only a few stragglers have occurred, the last over 80 years ago. A scheme to reintroduce the species was put into operation in 1970 when the Great Bustard Trust was founded at the instigation of the Hon. A.D. Tryon to mark International Conservation Year and with the single aim of re-establishing the Great Bustard as a native English breeding species. The largest flocks ever recorded in Britain were to be seen in growing crops on the perimeter of the Plain in winter. It seemed appropriate therefore that a site, in the region, should be found where the birds could be safely kept and propagated. After negotiations, the Ministry of Defence generously agreed to lease ten acres of ideal grassland in a secluded corner of Porton Down, and in due course the Trust built a large fox-proof pen to accommodate the Bustards. Young birds were brought in from Portugal, but the very first specimen was a wild female from East Germany which arrived, exhausted, on Fair Isle in January 1970. All the birds were pinioned and then turned loose in the pen. They are regularly fed but have reverted to their original shyness and react to humans in the same way as wild birds. The current stock consists of four males and four females and it is hoped that they will breed, and that any offspring will eventually colonise the surrounding downland.

Stone Curlews are becoming scarcer, undoubtedly due largely to modern farming methods with increased mechanisation which destroys the nests or disturbs sitting birds. In spite of this a few pairs breed every summer. On still evenings their haunting cries can be heard – particularly at dusk – but often well into the night. The birds flock up in autumn and have been seen right into the latter half of October.

Cultivated areas on the periphery of the Plain attract many species. Skylarks, which breed on the ranges in summer and are perhaps the commonest bird, form flocks in winter and parties of more than a hundred frequent the stubbles – Mallard also take advantage of this source of food and flight in at dusk for their share of the "gleanings". Mixed flocks, including Chaffinch,, Yellowhammer and Brambling with occasional Reed Bunting frequent the plough: the Brambling will tend to favour the vicinity of beech stands where they search for beech-mast. Goldfinches also build up flocks in winter and the seeds of stemless thistles and weeds form the main source of food. Another typical bird of the Plain is the Corn Bunting which can be heard "jangling" from a barbed wire fence or gate post throughout the day in spring and even sometimes in winter. Stock Doves nest regularly in derelict tanks and Wheatears have been found nesting in old smoke-shell cases.

As mentioned previously this account deals with the "cap" of the Plain which consists in the main of military ranges of varying physical features which may be summarised as follows.

Imber Ranges have vast areas of grassland criss-crossed by tank tracks which form natural nesting sites for ground nesting birds such as Lapwings; water tends to lie in these depressions in winter which attracts flocks of Linnets. The village, which is now derelict with crumbling buildings, has shrubs and trees in what remains of once pretty cottage gardens, and these provide a variety of habitats and ideal sites for Spotted Flycatchers, House Martins, Swallows etc. (Strangely enough there are no House Sparrows on Imber Ranges.) The odd ruined farm buildings dotted about on these ranges also make excellent nesting sites for Jackdaws and owls.

West Down Artillery Range has huge areas of grassland without tank tracks and disturbed ground, but on impact regions the grass is frequently burnt and these zones are, of course, inaccessible. The grassland is more uniform than that found on Imber – *Zerna erecta* being the dominant species – and this more scanty ground cover is less suitable for small mammals, resulting in fewer birds of prey hunting over the area. There are few trees – mostly blasted by shell fire, but some woods near the perimeter are favoured by passerines, woodpeckers etc. Gorse and hawthorn grow mainly in the north.

Larkhill Artillery Range, which incorporates West Down, is bounded by the A360 road on the west and by the A345 on the east and consists of great rolling areas of grassland dotted with a few mature woods of fir and beech where woodpeckers breed, and the undergrowth is ideal for the smaller passerines. There are also some recently established plantations consisting mainly of Scots Pine planted about twenty years ago and a mixture of deciduous and fir trees planted during the last ten years. Small areas near Blackball Firs and Newfoundland Farm have been ploughed and regularly cultivated, the rest is either grazed by cattle, cut for hay or lying fallow. This means that most of the downland turf has remained undisturbed for at least seventy years. Short-eared Owls find this area of rough grass attractive as do Merlins and other falcons. The impact areas, on the other hand, support very little in the way of trees apart from a few bare stumps and small clumps of thorn scrub and gorse and the bird life consists mainly of Skylarks and pipits with a few Whinchats.

Bulford Ranges have more varied habitats, with short grass on the small arms ranges frequented by members of the thrush family. The woodland is of various ages consisting largely of conifers, in which raptors breed, and there is an area of mixed scrub and juniper in the south favoured by Whinchats and Tree Pipits. To the north in the region of Haxton Down it opens out into typical downland grassland which in winter is hunted over by Hen Harriers and Short-eared Owls with an occasional Merlin and even more rarely a Peregrine. The odd Barn Owl is resident and from time to time a Tawny Owl will establish a territory. Sidbury Hill, 735 feet (224 m.), is the highest point on these otherwise fairly low ranges and is a favourite haunt of warblers in summer while in winter Redpolls may be found.

None of the ranges has streams or permanent ponds, but water does lie in some of the old dew ponds and other suitable hollows for a time, especially after prolonged heavy rain. The only other sources of water are the occasional cattle trough and dew.

Finally, together with the New Forest, Dartmoor and Exmoor, Salisbury Plain provides one of the few remaining large areas of undisturbed natural habitat for wild life in the South West of the British Isles.

THE SALISBURY AVON

by Martin Peers

THE Salisbury Avon – like the Hampshire chalk rivers Test and Itchen – is famed for the clarity of its water and has a very shallow gradient. It rises in the Vale of Pewsey, from which three streams flow southwards to converge at Rushall. The river then cuts through the chalk of Salisbury Plain until it reaches Amesbury. From here, it winds its way slowly through wooded hills before skirting the historic Roman and Norman fortress of Old Sarum, to be joined in the new city by the Nadder and the Wylye below the dominant spire of the beautiful cathedral. Below the city the Bourne joins the main river near Petersfinger, while the Ebble flows in from the picturesque Chalke Valley near Longford Castle. As the river broadens on its way to the coast at Christchurch, the valley becomes much more open with a large and level bottom.

In addition to the river's undoubted importance as a wetland ornithological site, the sides of its great valley also contribute in no small way to its significance. In particular, the woodland slopes at Trafalgar and on the eastern flank of the great Clarendon Estate are favoured haunts of the Buzzard, which can be watched in all months of the year. These slopes include patches of damp woodland, which provide nesting sites for the elusive Willow Tit and Lesser Spotted Woodpecker. Here and there, where suitable thickets are found (as at Shootend), are Nightingales, but the Redstarts have all but vanished, apart from the occasional migrant in spring and autumn. Other typical woodland species are well represented in these areas.

The more open sides of the valley are predominantly farmland with a few areas of downland or scrub. As with the woodland, these areas have most of the species of nesting birds which one would expect to find: Kestrels, Little Owls, Skylarks, Corn Buntings, Turtle Doves, Whitethroats, Lapwings, Yellowhammers, Partridges and Cuckoos are all well represented, while Barn Owls and Lesser Whitethroats are slightly more localised. A typically good area for breeding birds is to be found at Clearbury Ring near Charlton-All-Saints. In addition, Clearbury, along with other prominent sites such as Haxton, Old Sarum and Standlynch Down are important at times of passage. Wheatears move along the tops and in autumn especially flocks of Lapwing, Golden Plover, Black-headed and other gulls, winter thrushes and finches, pipits and Skylarks move down the valley sides. Golden Plover flocks gather regularly at certain places – particularly Netheravon, Old Sarum and Charlton – with flocks reaching large numbers (such as c. 2,000 at Charlton in February 1978). Gull flocks are dominated by Black-headed (with 1,000 + a typical count for the Downton to Britford area at peak times) although all five common species may be represented, including the odd Great Black-backed on occasion. Rarer records include a Whimbrel at Old Sarum in July 1977, a Ring Ouzel at Clearbury in September 1977, Corncrakes above Charlton in three autumns between 1963 and 1969, and four Arctic Skuas flying south over Little Durnford in September 1976. Winter raptors have included Hen Harriers on Clearbury Ring.

The Woodford Valley is a particularly beautiful and unspoilt section of the Avon system. Here the river meanders slowly between Amesbury and the more open flat-bottomed valley area at Stratford-sub-Castle. Breeding water birds include good numbers of Little Grebe, Mallard, Coot, Moorhen and Mute Swan. Tufted Duck may be seen at most times of the year, particularly near Great Durnford, but their numbers increase in winter, when they are joined occasionally by a few Pochard; two pairs of Goldeneye were seen near the bridge at Middle Woodford in February 1978.

Occasionally, the more wooded sides give way to damp waterside meadows, the breeding ground for several pairs of Redshanks (as at Durnford) and the odd pair of Snipe (particularly near Stratford). At the latter site, a few pairs of Yellow Wagtails also breed. Other waterside species include Sedge Warblers which are locally common (as at Great Durnford), a few pairs of Reed Warblers where there are suitable *Phragmites* beds, Reed Buntings, Kingfishers and Grey Wagtails, while Herons make regular appearances at the river's edge. Rarer birds observed near Stratford in the breeding season are most likely to be escapes from F.R.H. Swann's wildfowl collection and include such exotic species as Bar-headed Goose,

Carolina Duck, Red-crested Pochard and Pintail. Autumn and winter sightings of unusual species are more likely to be genuine: a Greenshank in September 1976 at Stratford; a Bittern near Amesbury in the winter of 1978-9, are two such reports worth mentioning here. Finally, winter wader numbers near Stratford and Woodford include up to fifty Snipe and several Woodcock; among these flocks, Teal are often seen – usually in small numbers between Stratford and Little Durnford, or else nearer West Amesbury.

The city of Salisbury is remarkably good for bird-watching. It may be the only urban area in Britain to have had breeding Stone Curlews within its boundary during the last ten years. There cannot be many other cities, either, which boast breeding birds such as Barn Owl, Redshank, Stonechat and Nightingale! The riverside areas are particularly worth conserving since they are relatively unspoilt by the over-efficiency of modern farming or the pollution of industrial waste. Let us hope that the people of Salisbury give determined support to the C.P.R.E. in its fight to preserve quiet backwaters against those who would develop them for industry and housing, as has happened to the detriment of other places.

Some good waterside habitat, with selections of typical breeding species may be seen between Bemerton and Harnham by the rivers Nadder and Wylye. However, in relation to the Avon, perhaps the two most important Salisbury sites are those between Stratford-sub-Castle and the City Ring Road, together with the meadows by the river at Town Path below the Cathedral. The former of these two habitats can be viewed by crossing the Avon by the footbridge at Stratford, before following the footpath on the Devizes Road side of the river towards the city via allotments and waterside meadows. It is possible that part of this habitat – a very marshy and scrubby field which contained several breeding pairs of Reed and Sedge Warblers, together with three pairs of Reed Buntings, a pair of Grasshopper Warblers, and (in 1976 at least) one pair of Stonechats – has already been reclaimed for allotments. However the *Phragmites* beds on the opposite side of the river remain for other Reed Warblers, and several pairs of Yellow Wagtails, which breed in the wet meadows used for cattle, also feed in the allotments. The river itself at this point contains breeding Little

Grebe, Mallard, Moorhen and Mute Swan: many of these birds come to feed in the centre of the city itself.

The meadows which lie due west of the Cathedral are famous since Constable depicted them in the early nineteenth century. A footpath, called "Town Path", which starts in the City, crosses here to Harnham and provides splendid views over this memorable scene. The junctions of Nadder and Wylye skirt the northwestern edge before being joined from the north by the Avon; thence the river passes the Cathedral on its way to Britford. The river has breeding Little Grebe, Mallard, Moorhen, Mute Swan, Kingfisher, and – in concrete pipes beside the river here – as at Salisbury Car Park – a small colony of Sand Martins. Three species of wagtail can be seen by the river or in the meadows used by feeding cattle, with at least three pairs of Yellow Wagtails breeding. Waders include Lapwing and Redshank, while small wisps of Snipe are sometimes flushed in the winter months. A tame Water Rail spent several winters in the early 1970s in a ditch beside the Town Path, delighting many people with good views. Rank vegetation with occasional beds of *Phragmites* attract Sedge and Reed Warblers together with Reed Buntings: all three species frequent the meadows and the bottom of gardens in Salisbury Close which border the river's edge. Hawfinches have been noted in the Close and in the winter months Siskins are a not uncommon sight here – as indeed they are at one or two other Salisbury sites with alder and birch. Passage of migrating Swifts and hirundines can be heavy just here, particularly in the early morning or late evening. Indeed, first thing in the morning is the time to visit Town Path, before the bustle of shoppers interrupts the placid serenity of a landscape disturbed only by birdsong, a flash of turquoise, a hovering Kestrel or a quartering Barn Owl.

About a mile or so to the south of the Cathedral, a pollarded willow provides a nesting site for a pair of Barn Owls on the opposite bank to the gravel pits at Petersfinger. These small pools were featured in an attractive television production called "The Petersfinger Cuckoo". Although used for much of the year by anglers, these old pits provide a needed site for birds at all seasons. Great Crested Grebe have bred on occasion, as also may have Tufted Duck; the other commonly nesting water birds are also here. Beside the pools, the scrub, *Phragmites* and other rank vegetation including reeds provide a nesting place for Blackcap, Chiffchaff, Willow, Reed and Sedge Warbler. In the winter months, duck are not particularly numerous save at dusk when they congregate, but Tufted Duck are usually present and Pochard occasionally occur; in cold spells – as in 1956 and December 1976 – Goosander have been recorded, as was Long-tailed Duck in October 1950.

Across the Avon from Petersfinger lie the Britford water-meadows. The warming conditions created by the water-meadows make them particularly attractive to birds in cold weather. Like those a few miles downstream at Standlynch, near Charlton-All-Saints, these meadows were originally intended to increase agricultural productivity by periodic flooding. In the colder months, the main river attracts birds such as Little Grebe, Coot and Kingfisher, while Grey Wagtails prefer the sluice-gates and Dippers have been recorded on occasion. The very broad stretch of deep water at Charlton is attractive to diving ducks (notably Pochard and Tufted Duck), which are there in small numbers annually. Sometimes they are joined by one or two Gadwall or Great Crested Grebe and possibly the odd Goldeneye. In the adjacent watermeadows here – as at Britford – flocks of Wigeon and Teal winter annually, the former usually numbering between 150 and 300, while the latter rarely exceed 100; Mallard peak earlier – in September – and numbers often reach 300 or more. Moorhens and Mute Swans form smaller flocks but other wildfowl are less common, with perhaps a few Shoveler or Pintail on occasion at Standlynch. Bewick's Swans occasionally stay for a few days on their way to or from Ibsley; White-fronted Geese also fly overhead annually en route to the same destination.

Wintering waders may not be so predictable as the Wigeon and Teal population but Water Rail, Snipe and Green Sandpipers occur annually, with Snipe often exceeding 50 in number at both Britford and Standlynch, particularly on frosty mornings. Other waders are brought in by cold weather and include Redshank, Dunlin and Ruff as well as rarer species. "Regulars" at this time of year include Cormorants (up to 15 have been recorded but numbers are usually lower than 10), the resident Herons, several species of gull, and – possibly regularly at Britford – Water Pipits, which were noted in the winter of

1977-8. Other winter visitors occur in unpredictable numbers depending on the proximity of suitable feeding areas – Fieldfares, Redwings, Stonechats and Meadow Pipits fairly regularly, with Bramblings, Redpolls and Tree Sparrows more erratically. Bitterns used to occur frequently in the Avon Valley during the winter months, especially at Britford, but few have been reported in recent years, though there was one at Charlton in 1973.

In the breeding season, both Charlton and Britford have good numbers of the common water and waterside species which have been mentioned elsewhere, with particularly good colonies of Reed and Sedge Warblers. In addition, there is a heronry containing about twenty pairs at Britford, while a single pair of Yellow Wagtails breeds near by. Both here and at Charlton, Grasshopper Warblers may be heard reeling during the summer months; an early morning visit may reveal at least two pairs each of Snipe and Redshank at both localities.

Although the Avon below Salisbury provides attractive nesting habitat for species such as Snipe and Redshank, which are becoming increasingly local, it is at passage times that its usefulness becomes particularly evident. Waterfowl and waders use the valley as a flyway, noticeably from autumn through to spring. As well as several species such as Wigeon, Teal and Dunlin mentioned above, there is a predictable movement of Canada Geese, Redshank, Snipe, Common and Green Sandpipers, with other species occurring more erratically, like Curlew, Black-tailed Godwit, Greenshank and Shelduck. "Commic" and Black Terns probably also occur fairly regularly at favoured locations such as Shootend, Longford Castle, or the broadwater at Charlton. From the valley bottom – especially the footpath across the watermeadows at Britford – a considerable migration of Swifts and hirundines may be watched; it was here, on 2nd October, 1977, that there was a passage of 72 Jays flying west in less than three hours. Other passage species, both over the valley and through the vegetation at the bottom, have included Osprey, Hobby, Merlin, various pipits, warblers and finches. More systematic observations would probably indicate a more definite pattern of movement.

To conclude, the Avon below Salisbury flows through some of the least altered landscape in South Wiltshire. This has enabled it to support a good number of representative breeding species as well as providing an important habitat for migrating and wintering birds. The whole valley needs protection from development, but particularly the water meadows which are vital to an area of predominantly dry chalkland. It is to be hoped that future generations will inherit as unspoilt a landscape from us as we have from Constable and our forefathers.

THE VALE OF WARDOUR

by Jack Major

THE area of Wiltshire of which I write is that part which lies south of a line drawn from Mere through Great Ridge Wood to Wilton. It is roughly elliptical in shape, with the River Nadder flowing through it from west to east, while chalk hills lie parallel on either side. Tributaries of the Sem and Nadder subdivide it, and plateaux, ridges and outcrops of sandstone, some overlaid with greensand, upset the simple pattern. There is heavy clay in the valleys. The chalk hills to the south are steeper than those to the north, and therefore include a greater proportion of land that has escaped the plough and so has retained its native grasses, wild flowers and insects associated with these. The great expanses of downland, once sheep-walks, that stretch towards Tollard Royal, Alvediston and beyond, are now permanent, flinty arable. Some steep hillsides still support natural mixed woodland, some have thorn or elder scrub, and some only thin turf. The relics of yew trees, destroyed by explosive, date the introduction of cattle to these slopes c. 1945.

The characteristic bird is, or ought to be, the Stone Curlew, and until the mid-sixties a few returned each year to their favourite fields. It also occurred near Mere and in fair numbers on the fringe of Great Ridge Wood; but now it comes no more though, a few miles away in Dorset, it certainly bred as recently as 1976. The related Lapwing also breeds on these flinty uplands, though in reduced numbers, but in lowland pastures that are now better drained it has become scarce.

As lately as the mid-fifties the Wheatear was a common summer resident on these bare valley sides; on Chilmark Down, now a uniform plain of growing corn, and elsewhere on the Great Ridge it used to be numerous, but now, even where the habitat remains suitable, it is to be seen only on passage. Only fifteen years ago the Redstart was to be found in copses and elder scrub, even in very thin scrub; I once found five nests within a mile. It also appeared in woodland where old trees had been left standing. But it must now be classed as a rare visitor.

A male was in song in Fonthill Woods in May, 1980, however. Once only have I seen a Black Redstart; this was on 10th May 1965, on White Sheet Hill.

Many sightings over the years have persuaded me that Hobbies breed in the area, though (perhaps for want of persistence) I have never found a nest. A few pairs of Barn Owls survive away from trunk roads, where so many are killed, and away from total agriculture, with its lack of old trees and permanent, mouse-harbouring pasture. Pellets cast by one pair which lived on the edge of a vast Starling roost at The Grove, Wardour, consisted largely of Starlings' skulls. Of the other owls the Long-eared, also largely dependent on a good supply of rodents, no longer exists here, but the Tawny Owl seems to maintain its numbers. Once, in mid-June 1975, I had the unusual experience of watching one quartering large corn fields in broad daylight, like a harrier. The Little Owl, perhaps for lack of suitable nest sites, occurs but here and there.

The Kestrel remains common, breeding mainly in old nests of the Corvidae, particularly on downland. The Sparrowhawk, even in the period of full use of chlorinated hydrocarbon pesticides, was never really scarce, and the planting of conifers, many of them now maturing, must benefit the species. One pair of Buzzards regularly occupies a territory in these chalklands, and I know of four other pairs at least. There were at least three confirmed breeding records in 1980, with another nest near Semley being robbed of eggs – probably by crows. One pair already had two eggs on 3 April 1968, an early date; this nest, and another in the same place ten years later, were garnished with larch twigs. Before the advent of myxomatosis the late C.R. Verner once found eleven occupied nests in a single year in Great Ridge Wood, but it is now much less numerous. In early spring, when noisy and conspicuous, it is easily shot by a vigilant keeper.

The years 1970 and 1971 were good Quail years, in which the birds could be heard calling from many cornfields on the chalk, especially near Hindon. The Red-legged Partridge, without being common, still outnumbers the Grey Partridge, and is sometimes to be seen in huge, combined coveys: I have counted thirty-five birds together. Perhaps it prospers through feeding mostly on uncultivated land.

On these hills the Skylark is still very common. But over the last ten years there has been a steady and marked decrease in the numbers of another small, ground-nesting bird, the Corn Bunting. At Charlton Down there was but a single cock bird present in 1978; the cause may be the rotary mower, or perhaps insecticides sprayed from the air. Stonechats, usually alone, are occasionally seen on rough ground in late autumn, and single Whinchats occur on migration; I have no evidence of either species breeding. Two or three pairs of Tree Pipits are to be found each year in open patches on Semley Common, and the Wood Warbler has bred here and was to be heard in 1980, both here and in Fonthill Woods. It seems to be represented by apparently unmated cocks. But there is too much disturbance from motor-cycle scramblers for the Nightjar to remain. At the northern end of Donhead Clift lies Oyster Coppice, a small wet wood so called because a great quantity of oyster shells was once found here, a relic, perhaps, of a Roman picnic. Here, in 1963, when there was still snow on the ground, I came across the incomplete boring for a Willow Tit's nest; later, this was completed, and a nest was made in the same tree in the following year. Since then I have seen some thirty nests from Haddon Hill, near East Knoyle, to Haredene Wood beyond Tisbury. Alder, Hazel and Sallow are the trees most commonly used for the nest-hole in this area, but almost anything that decays to the consistency of Balsa wood may be used. Stems of no more than three inches in diameter are used, where the walls of the nest chamber are composed of little more than the bark. Nightingales have decreased recently, and the last I heard were near Gutch Common in 1973 and at Summerhaze Oaks a year later: both birds were probably unmated.

At the head of the River Nadder, near Ludwell, a pair of Dippers has recently been reported in a site where they formerly bred; elsewhere, except for a single site at Fonthill, they are uncommon. The Kingfisher has bred in the banks of the Sem but is unlikely to be found much above Tisbury; but further downstream it occurs more regularly. Once to my knowledge the Grey Wagtail has bred beside the muddy, sluggish waters of the Sem in Semley village; but it breeds beside sluices and rapids all along the Nadder and its tributaries. The Common Sandpiper is regularly seen during the spring migration beside these streams and by Fonthill Lake. The Wood Sandpiper has been seen rarely, in late July, usually by ditches and rivulets in ordinary farmland.

On Semley Common cattle were last put out generally in 1969, and there were a few in 1970. Casualties and thefts then put an end to the practice. Within a year or two local farmers began to cut and bale the coarse grass on the Common, where, until then, a few pairs of Reed Bunting and Grasshopper Warbler used to breed, and even an occasional Sedge Warbler in a wet corner. The Cuckoo also found a good feeding ground here, with the Dunnock as the usual foster-parent.

Between Wilton and Harnham, in the Nadder Valley, there used to be a large expanse of rushy water meadows: here Redshank, Snipe and Yellow Wagtail would breed. But now the whole area is ordinary pasture, and it is unlikely that any of these remain. But Redshank and Snipe still breed in the Avon Valley south of Salisbury, where the Snipe are shot in winter. In this region the Lesser Spotted Woodpecker is more frequent than elsewhere, perhaps because of the abundance of old decaying willows. In the same area, near Quidhampton, a nest of the Water Rail was found in 1972: the eggs were taken by boys.

During the last eighteen years several small rookeries have disappeared, and also at least three larger ones at Pertwood, Ashcombe and on the ox drove near Berwick St. John. There has been no noticeable increase in neighbouring rookeries, nor have new ones been established. The trees were respectively Beech, Sycamore (for the most part) and Scots Pine. There has been evidence of a slow, long-term decline in the numbers of the Rook.

Two pairs of Herons nested in Berry Wood Copse, near Donhead, in 1977 and since there were two old nests close by, the colony was probably established in the previous year. In 1978 there were seven occupied nests, but before the year's end felling of all the spindly birches and alders had begun. A single pair of Herons also reared young in a very low nest at Wardour in 1976. Apart from the Mallard the only resident duck is the Tufted Duck, on Fonthill Lake. In 1974 several pairs of Pochard from the wintering parties stayed on into May, and perhaps bred.

The Whitethroat has not regained its numbers since the crash of 1969, and most cocks heard on arrival move on again soon afterwards, as if unmated. A few pairs of Lesser Whitethroats turn up from time to time. The Tree Sparrow is scarcer here than in the north of the county, and first came to my notice in 1964 when three or four pairs were using old woodpecker borings by the River Nadder. Two years later the Water Board tidied up the banks of the river, and removed the rotten alders, but one pair remained and used a nest-box on a sound tree. In 1972 a pair built a nest in a small, dense, much-browsed hawthorn bush near Hindon, at a height of only 3' 6" above ground. Two years later a new nest was built upon the vestiges of this nest, perhaps by the same bird. In 1974 I found a busy colony at a barn in Monkton Deverill, and when I put up nest-boxes the following year these were occupied within a week. This colony remained at strength until 1978 when, perhaps because of the severe weather in February, it was much reduced.

Somerford Common.

PLATE I

Old oak wood, Savernake Forest.

Beech wood, Savernake Forest.

PLATE III

Great Ridge Wood.

Oak standards and hazel coppice, Vernditch Chase.

PLATE V

Cotswold Water Park. Partially flooded sand pit. PLATE VI

Cotswold Water Park. Upper Waterhay Farm. PLATE VII

Cotswold Water Park. Gravel pit, flooded after working. Oaksey.

PLATE VIII

Coate Water, Swindon: in summer.

PLATE IX

Coate Water, Swindon: in winter.

Calne sand pits. Sand Martin colony.

PLATE XI

River Avon, near Lacock.

PLATE XII

Valley of By Brook above Castle Combe.

PLATE XIII

By Brook above Castle Combe.

By Brook above Castle Combe.

PLATE XV

By Brook above Castle Combe.

River Avon, Flood meadows, Lower Seagry, summer. PLATE XVII

River Kennet. Old water meadows, Axford. PLATE XVIII

Shalbourne, watercress beds.

PLATE XIX

Ladywell, Imber Ranges.

PLATE XX

South Down Farm, Imber Ranges.

PLATE XXI

Downs near Calston. PLATE XXII

Fifield Down National Nature Reserve.

PLATE XXIII

Porton Down. PLATE XXIV

Sutton Down, near Prescombe.

PLATE XXV

Kennet and Avon Canal, North Horton.

River Kennet, between Ramsbury and Axford.

PLATE XXVII

Steple Langford, lakes.

Kennet and Avon Canal, New Mill, N.E. of Pewsey.

PLATE XXIX

River Avon, Water meadows, Britford.

PLATE XXX

River Avon Valley, between Downton and Salisbury.

PLATE XXXI

Fonthill Lake.

PLATE XXXII

SYSTEMATIC LIST

by Geoffrey Webber

INTRODUCTION

THE systematic list that follows is divided into two parts. Part 1 lists all the species that have bred within the county boundary although some have not done so for a number of years. Part 2 contains all the non-breeding visitors to the county and, so far as is known, is complete to the end of 1979, with a few additions for 1980.

A large proportion of the breeding data is based on information obtained during the years 1968-72 when fieldwork for the British Trust for Ornithology's *"Atlas of Breeding Birds in Britain and Ireland"* was being carried out. For the majority of species this information has been up-dated to the breeding season of 1979 and a few 1980 records of particular importance are also included.

Maps are provided for selected species, particularly those having a restricted distribution, but are excluded for the less common and vulnerable ones.

The lists follow the sequence and nomenclature of Professor Dr. K.H. Voous adopted by 'The "British Birds" List of Birds of the Western Palearctic'.

PART ONE — BREEDING BIRDS

LITTLE GREBE *Tachybaptus ruficollis*

Resident.

Widely distributed and breeding in 27 of the 10 km. squares. It breeds on both of the Rivers Avon including their major tributaries, being commoner on the Salisbury Avon. The River Kennet supports a number of pairs from Marlborough in the west to the county boundary in the east.

Suitable stretches of the Kennet and Avon Canal are also used, particularly in the Great Bedwyn area. The Thames and its tributaries are much less popular with only a few pairs attempting to breed on the Rivers Cole, Ray and Swillbrook.

Breeding has been attempted on most of the larger lakes and gravel pits with varying success. Most of these lakes tend to have small flocks during the winter months.

GREAT CRESTED GREBE *Podiceps cristatus*

Resident and summer visitor.

Until the early years of this century it was a very rare visitor. Smith could list only four records for the nineteenth century.

Breeding was first confirmed at Coate Water in 1913 and had probably taken place there the previous year. The county was then slowly colonised via Braydon Pond, Shearwater and Westbury Ponds.

In 1939, 21 pairs were counted on nine waters and the 1931 census showed a similar total from 11 waters. Numbers remained at about the same level until the war years when they began to increase. The 1965 census provided a total of 34 pairs from 17 waters and the results of the 1975 census are shown below.

	No. of pairs		*No. of pairs*
Bowood Lake	4	Lacock Gravel Pit	1
Braydon Pond	1	Shearwater	2
Coate Water	7	Steeple Langford	2
Corsham Lake	3	Stourton Lake	3
Erlestoke Lake	1	Tockenham Reservoir	1
Gasper Lake	1	Westbury Ponds	3

Cotswold Water Park 9 (six different pits being used)

Total: 38 pairs

As yet there have been no attempts to breed on rivers in the county although some stretches of the Thames and Salisbury Avon might be suitable. In mild winters loose flocks build up on some of the larger waters and decrease rapidly with the onset of hard weather. Numbers at Coate Water seldom exceed 40 and smaller flocks occur in the Water Park.

An adult ringed at Morden, Surrey in February 1965 was found dead at Stanton Fitzwarren in February 1966.

GREY HERON *Ardea cinerea*

Resident.

The fortunes of the Heron in Wiltshire have fluctuated during the past ninety years but until recently they have tended to increase.

In 1887 Smith listed the following heronries:

Crouch Wood, Highworth	c. 25	occupied nests
Bowood	15	" "
Savernake	6	" "
Longleat	c. 12	" "
Fonthill	8	" "
Compton Park	12	" "
Longford	c. 6	" "

The above total of 84 occupied nests had fallen to c. 60 by 1928, the Crouch Wood and Longford sites being deserted, but new colonies had been established at Bradford Wood and Somerford Brook.

In 1957 eleven heronries produced c. 65 nests, a small increase during the 29 years. The next decade saw a further increase even though 1962/63 was an extremely hard winter. The total of occupied nests in 1967 was 71 from eight heronries.

During the seventies numbers rose rapidly to a peak of 142 nests in 1974. Reasons for this increase remain obscure but a succession of mild winters was certainly an important factor. Since then there has been a decline to 107 nests in 1976 and 100 in 1978. The sites in use during 1978 are listed below:

Great Bradford Wood	20 occupied nests
Ashton Keynes	12 " "
Bathampton House	3 " "
Bowood	11 " "
Boyton	10 " "
Britford	5 " "
Longford	10 " "
Savernake	21 " "
Hillocks Wood	7 " "
West Tytherton	1 " "

A bird ringed at Clairmarais, Pas-de-Calais, France in May 1955 was recovered at Chippenham in April 1956.

MUTE SWAN *Cygnus olor*

Resident.

This species occurs throughout the county wherever suitable stretches of water are available. The three British Trust for Ornithology enquiries give an accurate account of the species' status.

	1955		1961		1978	
Locality	*Breeding pairs*	*Non-breeding pairs*	*Breeding pairs*	*Non-breeding pairs*	*Breeding pairs*	*Non-breeding pairs*
Avon (Bristol)	9	2	6	39	5	44
Marden, Biss, By Brook	3		1		1	
Thames, Cole and Ray	2	22	2	19	10	27
Kennet and Avon Canal	11	16	13	30	9	11
Kennet and Og	4	55	10	64	5	35
Avon (Salisbury)	33	52	31	45	41	153
Wylye	13	97	25	134	16	25
Till	1		2		2	
Nadder	1		8	59	13	18
Ebble			2		1	
Bourne	3		6			
Lakes, ponds & gravel pits	37	30	22	74	31	71
Totals	117	274	128	464	134	384

The table above lists all the birds located during the breeding seasons of 1955, 1961 and 1978. The localities are divided into major river systems with all the lakes, ponds and gravel pits grouped together.

Birds holding territory but not providing definite proof of breeding are included in the non-breeding total.

GREYLAG GOOSE *Anser anser*

Vagrant and feral breeder.

There was a single record for the last century, two birds being shot from a flock at Sutton Benger in 1838. The four records for this century up to 1975 may well refer to escapes from captivity.

During the winter of 1975/76 a small flock arrived in the Cotswold Water Park and a feral breeding population has become established. Breeding has taken place in Wiltshire on two occasions. The original colonists apparently escaped from a local collection in Gloucestershire.

CANADA GOOSE *Branta canadensis*

Resident, introduced.

Prior to 1900 this species bred only in captivity and there were very few records of birds in a feral state. Although a number of introductions were made during the first half of the century feral breeding was not recorded until 1968. In that year a pair was seen with two goslings at Wilton Water. Two pairs attempted to breed at the same site in 1969, and breeding continues to date. By 1970 several pairs were in residence along the Kennet east of Marlborough and goslings were seen on a gravel pit near Ashton Keynes. Two new sites were used in 1974, single pairs breeding at Stanton Fitzwarren and Lacock, both these sites being in regular occupation. In 1977 the flock in the Kennet valley exceeded 150 individuals with all suitable sites being occupied by pairs in the breeding season. In the same year two pairs attempted to breed at Coate Water where one pair had reared goslings in the previous year. Meanwhile the Cotswold Water Park breeding population has slowly been building up but all recent breeding records have been in Gloucestershire.

The steady increase in the breeding population has resulted in an increase of sight records well away from the regular breeding areas.

TEAL *Anas crecca*

Winter visitor, has bred.

A widespread but recently decreasing winter visitor. From the winters 1949/50 to 1962/63 the highest monthly Wildfowl Count total was 417 with maximum figures for most winters approaching this figure. Since then only one count has exceeded 100, the majority being well below this total. One major reason for the decline could be the restoration of higher water levels at Coate Water by 1964/65. Previously flocks at this site regularly attained totals of 300 but now seldom reach double figures.

It can usually be found in ones and twos on most freshwater marshes and on those larger waters with suitable cover during the winter months.

There are a very few breeding records, the most recent being in 1969 near the Salisbury Avon, and a nest was found near Chilton Foliat in 1976.

MALLARD *Anas platyrhynchos*

Resident.

Widespread and common, breeding in all the 10 km. squares. Since 1954/55 the Wildfowl Counts have, with a few exceptions, shown a steady increase in the numbers of wintering birds. This increase has also been noted in the breeding population but with insufficient evidence to give an accurate total. There are breeding pairs on all the larger waters, these birds apparently being completely sedentary. In August and early September numbers rise on these waters presumably due to adults and young from surrounding farmland moving back to their winter quarters. A further increase takes place in October, the birds involved apparently being migrants from further afield. During hard weather there are fluctuations in numbers but the majority appear to be content to wait for conditions to improve. Ringing returns show movement between the county and Belgium, Holland and Germany.

Hand-reared birds are still released, notably at Bowood, and feeding takes place at a number of sites.

The maximum counts at major waters for 1967/68 and 1977/78 were as follows:

Locality	*1967/68*	*1977/78*
Bowood Lake	900	487
Braydon Pond	116	19
Coate Water	295	245
Corsham Lake	125	78
Chilton Foliat	58	172
Erlestoke Lake	12	5
Fonthill Lake	224 (1969/70)	227
Longleat	69	72
Lacock gravel pit	20	18
Ramsbury	700	490
Steeple Langford	60	220
Shearwater	40	136
Wilton Water	50	136

Counts for the Cotswold Water Park began in 1970/71 but were not differentiated on a county basis until recently.

SHOVELER *Anas clypeata*

Winter visitor, has bred.

There are two reasonably well documented breeding records, at Salisbury in 1946 and on the county boundary near Ashton Keynes in 1972. Pairs have summered at other sites but without actual proof of breeding.

Numbers in winter tend to fluctuate, normally being at a maximum in December and January. Flocks frequently reach double figures but only occasionally exceed 20. Most of the larger waters hold some birds in winter with Corsham Lake a popular site, and recently numbers have increased at Coate Water with up to 40 in late 1978. Freshwater marshes and sewage farms are frequently used during migration periods. After the winter peak there is often a small secondary peak in late March as returning migrants pass through.

Wildfowl Counts for major waters in 1967/68 and 1977/78 were:

Locality	*1967/68*	*1977/78*
Coate Water	1	14
Corsham Lake	1	9
Fonthill Lake	4 (1969/70)	4
Lacock gravel pit	2	
Ramsbury		1
Shearwater		1
Steeple Langford		10
Wilton Water	3	

RED-CRESTED POCHARD *Netta rufina*

Resident and uncommon visitor.

This species remained unrecorded in the county until December 1954 when a single male was seen at Braydon Pond. Four more were recorded during the following ten years since when it has been a regular winter visitor in ones and twos.

In 1974 a pair bred in the Poole Keynes area of the Water Park and subsequently a small breeding population has built up. During the winter these birds are frequently seen on the Ashton Keynes pits within the county. A duck was seen on one of these pits in 1976 accompanied by ducklings, all of which fell victim to unidentified predators.

The origins of this population are unknown but since this species is easily bred in captivity it probably derives from escapes.

POCHARD *Aythya ferina*

Winter visitor, has bred.

This species is a regular winter visitor normally arriving in mid-October and departing in March with stragglers into April. A very few individuals summer and there are six breeding records: single broods at Clarendon Lake in 1962 and 1965; two females with broods, Corsham Lake 1979, single broods at Steeple Langford and Shearwater also in 1979.

Wildfowl Counts for major waters in 1967/68 and 1977/78 were as follows:

Locality	*1967/1968*	*1977/1978*
Bowood Lake	4	6
Braydon Pond		10
Coate Water	18	62
Corsham Lake	26	26
Chilton Foliat		27
Fonthill	44 (1969/70)	129
Longleat	34	33
Lacock gravel pit	2	4
Ramsbury	6	2
Shearwater	20	12
Steeple Langford	57	163
Wilton Water	18	23

In recent years numbers have tended to increase and the larger waters have flocks in the 40 to 60 range, with up to c. 275 in the Cotswold Water Park (Ashton Keynes pits).

Rivers are used by this species only in hard weather when small flocks may be seen on the Kennet, Salisbury Avon and Thames.

TUFTED DUCK *Aythya fuligula*

Resident and winter visitor.

This species is a fairly common winter visitor on most of the larger areas of standing water and the slower and wider reaches of the rivers. These winter visitors normally arrive in October and depart in March. The majority of flocks consist of from 15 to 40 birds but occasionally exceed 100 in the Cotswold Water Park. Numbers appear to be rising slowly both in winter and during the breeding season.

Breeding was first noted at Wilton Water in 1926 closely followed by one or two pairs on the Kennet at Chilton Foliat. This population remained relatively static for nearly 20 years. Around 1940 new areas were colonised, on the Kennet, on the Avon at Britford, at Clarendon Lake, Longleat and Shearwater Lakes. There was then little change in breeding numbers or distribution until the mid-1960s, although wintering flocks tended to increase in size particularly at sites where breeding had not taken place. Breeding began in the Wiltshire pits of the Cotswold Water Park during the mid-1960s and further expansion took place along the Kennet from Marlborough in the west to Hungerford in the east. Probably all suitable stretches of this river are now occupied during the breeding season.

During the 1970s the expansion continued with breeding being proved at Braydon Pond, Coate Water, Fonthill Lake and Tockenham Reservoir. There have been isolated breeding records for Corsham Lake, Petersfinger gravel pits and on the Wylye. Figures obtained during the 1976 breeding season suggested a total breeding population of c. 100 pairs.

Birds ringed in Finland, the Netherlands and at Abberton in Essex have been recovered within the county.

Wildfowl Counts for major waters in 1967/68 and 1977/78 were:

Locality	*1967/1968*	*1977/1978*
Bowood Lake	2	6
Braydon Pond	37	4
Coate Water	9	38
Corsham Lake	6	38
Chilton Foliat	74	89
Erlestoke		24
Fonthill Lake	62 (1969/70)	106
Longleat	59	105
Lacock gravel pit	2	3
Ramsbury	14	8
Shearwater	40	28
Steeple Langford	30	121
Wilton Water	14	53

RUDDY DUCK *Oxyura jamaicensis*

Vagrant, introduced, has bred.

First recorded in the county at Corsham Lake in December 1966 and subsequently in the winters of 1970, 1971, 1972, 1975, 1976, 1977, 1978 (a male remaining during summer). A party of six was present at Coate Water in January 1976 with a pair remaining well into spring; a single male was there in May 1978 and in May and June 1979. An immature was present in the Water Park near Ashton Keynes in March 1978 and an adult male in May 1979.

In 1977 a duck was seen escorting small ducklings at Tockenham Reservoir. Unfortunately the lake was partially drained in the late summer and it is not known whether the young fledged successfully.

RED KITE *Milvus milvus*

Vagrant, former resident.

Although this species has not bred regularly in the county since the eighteenth century it seemed proper that it should be included in this section. Pairs were still present in the county up to c. 1840 and may well have continued to breed in wilder areas. Single birds were shot in 1858 and 1864 at Longleat and another at Font-hill in 1896.

There have been only eight records this century, at Ashton Keynes in April 1951, Long Dean in April 1958, Pitton Marsh in March 1963, Weavern in March 1966, and over the Marlborough Downs from September 1969 until March 1970. This was probably the bird found "long dead" near Ramsbury early in June which had been ringed as a nestling in central Wales during June 1969. Singles were also seen at Bishopstone near Salisbury in August 1971, at Leigh Delamere in May 1975 and flying south over Wilton in August 1976.

MONTAGU'S HARRIER *Circus pygargus*

Summer visitor.

During the last century this species was apparently evenly distributed throughout the more open parts of the county and breeding took place where conditions were suitable, although in very small numbers.

Recent breeding records referred to central areas of Salisbury Plain and in the extreme south-east, south and south-west of the county. The last known breeding record concerned two pairs using traditional sites during 1953.

There have been sight records, mainly of single birds, in most years since 1953 but in gradually decreasing numbers.

SPARROWHAWK *Accipiter nisus*
Resident.

This species has been very much persecuted in the county with the result that numbers have been kept artificially low. During the World Wars numbers tended to increase and they remained at a high level after the second War until the late 1950s. At this time there was a serious decline due to the use of certain Organochlorines as pesticides. Numbers remained very low for the next five years but began to increase from the mid-1960s. Since then numbers have built up and are now approaching levels attained during the Second World War. Although few nests are found birds are seen carrying prey into suitable nesting areas during the summer and newly fledged young are commonly seen. During fieldwork for the BTO "Atlas of Breeding Birds" breeding was proved in 21 of the 10 km. squares and since then it has been found to breed in all but five of the squares.

One ringed at Everleigh in July 1957 was recovered in France in November 1957.

BUZZARD *Buteo buteo*
Resident.

During the first half of the last century it was considered common but by 1890 it had become quite rare. The decrease was caused primarily by shooting, mainly in the interest of game preservation. The less intensive keepering during the 1914/18 war resulted in birds moving back into the county probably from the south-west. Numbers remained very low until 1931 when a pair bred close to the county boundary in Hampshire and sight records in the south began to increase.

The first authenticated breeding records for this century were in 1946 when three pairs reared young and two other pairs most probably bred. In 1954 seven occupied nests were found and four other pairs showed evidence of breeding, this being the highest number of pairs recorded this century. There was a marked decrease in 1956 due to the effects of myxomatosis on the rabbit population and recovery was extremely slow. In 1977 four pairs were known to breed and at least two other areas were occupied during the breeding season.

In most autumns there is a marked influx and there is evidence to suggest that well defined routes are used to traverse the county. A series of watches along the northern escarpments of the Marlborough Downs and Salisbury Plain in August, September and October showed that Buzzards were migrating from east to west along them. Wintering birds are frequently seen on the Marlborough Downs and Ministry of Defence land in the centre, south-west and west of the county.

A Steppe Buzzard *B. buteo vulpinus* was shot at Everleigh in September 1864 and another showing characters of that race was seen at Buttermere in March 1975.

KESTREL *Falco tinnunculus*
Resident.

A common resident breeding in all the 10 km. squares. Records for the last century indicate that it was common and well distributed. There is some evidence of a decline early this century but numbers apparently quickly built up again to previous levels. During the late 1950s there was a marked decrease although this was less serious in Wiltshire than in some other parts of the country. Since the mid-1950s numbers have increased rapidly and this species is now enjoying its most successful period this century although early reports for 1979 suggest that there has been a dramatic fall in the number of breeding pairs following the very hard winter. Some of these reports also suggest that breeding success has been extremely high with broods of five and six young being reared. At its commonest in open country with scattered trees it also frequents low-lying farmland, motorway verges and open sites in larger towns. Breeding has taken place on buildings in both Salisbury and Swindon. One bird ringed as a chick at Everleigh was recovered four months later in France.

MERLIN *Falco columbarius*

Winter visitor, has bred.

A regular visitor to Salisbury Plain and other upland areas from late August to April. Single birds occasionally seen in the summer months usually prove to be immatures.

A nest was found in 1971 containing three eggs, which unfortunately were taken by a predator wearing climbing irons. The male and female birds were both seen and positively identified, the latter at the nest which was that of a Carrion Crow situated in a Scots Pine.

A pair of birds reported at another site subsequent to the above record were present throughout the breeding season and were seen carrying prey but no young were seen.

HOBBY *Falco subbuteo*

Summer visitor.

Probably less common now than in the previous century but it still breeds regularly and there are widespread sight records in all recent years.

Nests are found at some traditional sites every year but those of other pairs prove more difficult to find, the birds only being seen carrying food or feeding fledged young.

In most recent years between ten and fifteen pairs have been located and sight records indicate that possibly twice that number may be present. Five 10 km. squares had confirmed breeding records during fieldwork for the BTO "Atlas of Breeding Birds" and three more have been added since.

Most birds arrive in late April or early May and depart in late September and early October. The earliest date is 9th April 1952 and the latest 14th November 1936.

A nestling ringed in the county during July 1953 was recovered in September of the same year at Espinho, Portugal. Another nestling ringed in July 1976 was recovered in Belgium in July 1977.

PEREGRINE *Falco peregrinus*

Uncommon visitor.

A regular visitor during the last century but now an uncommon and irregular visitor, most often seen between October and March.

Breeding has been attempted on several occasions on Salisbury Cathedral. The first record involved two eggs being removed from a gutter on the tower in 1878. In 1896 two young were hatched and were taken. One was purchased by Col. R. Meinertzhagen and the other by the Hon. Gerald Lascelles. They again nested in the early 1930s.

BLACK GROUSE *Tetrao tetrix*

Previously bred.

Until 1820 it bred regularly in the south-east of the county with casual records elsewhere in the south. A few pairs may have lingered on until the middle of the century but it was extinct as a breeding bird by the end of it. The last record was of a single bird shot near Warminster in April 1906.

RED-LEGGED PARTRIDGE *Alectoris rufa*
Resident, introduced.

Uncommon in the last century it is now widespread and locally common, preferring dry well-drained soils such as chalk downland and the sandy gravels of the upper Thames. In these areas it apparently maintains its numbers without frequent introductions. In southern and central districts the true status is obscured by the introduction of captive bred birds often in large numbers.

The recent sequence of dry summers seems to have been favourable to this species leading to an increase in the number of fledged young.

GREY PARTRIDGE *Perdix perdix*
Resident.

Generally common and widespread but numbers tend to fluctuate from year to year and can drop dramatically after wet summers. It is also very sensitive to changes in land usage and modern farm practices.

There was a serious reduction in numbers during the late 1950s and recovery was very slow until recently. During the last five years there has been a welcome increase leading to much larger autumn coveys and recolonisation of some marginal habitats but, unfortunately, early 1979 reports suggest a marked drop in numbers in some areas after the hard weather early in the year.

QUAIL *Coturnix coturnix*
Summer visitor.

Previously a common summer visitor which occasionally over-wintered. It is now rather scarce but still faithful to a number of traditional sites where numbers fluctuate considerably, at least when determined by the number of calling males. There is some evidence that this may indicate a lack of females rather than any increase in total numbers. Calling birds are mainly recorded from rank grassland and cereal crops on sheltered downland slopes and valleys.

It seldom arrives before late May and only a few recent records are later than early September. Extreme dates are 17th March 1961 and 22nd October 1965.

PHEASANT *Phasianus colchicus*

Resident, introduced.

Widespread and locally common and breeds ferally but numbers are augmented by large introductions of captive bred birds every year.

SPOTTED CRAKE *Porzana porzana*

Vagrant, has bred.

Apparently a regular visitor in the last century and appears to have bred at Mere in 1881. A nest was cut out in a field of clover adjacent to a marsh on 14th June. An egg sent to "The Field" was identified as belonging to this species. The site would suggest Corncrake rather than Spotted Crake but there is considerable size difference between eggs of the two species although coloration may be similar.

There are only three recent reports, at Idmiston in June 1969 and at Corsham in August 1969 and in October 1971.

CORNCRAKE *Crex crex*

Summer visitor.

It was a common summer visitor during the last century. By 1906 it had become scarce, by 1915 rare and shortly afterwards only occasional. It was a little less rare during the 1930s but decreased again at the end of that decade.

There are only two breeding records for the 1950s and six others which suggest that breeding may have taken place.

Recently one sight record per year has been the average and it seems unlikely that breeding will begin again. Wintering birds were noted at Salisbury in December 1899 and at Chippenham in January 1954.

MOORHEN *Gallinula chloropus*
Resident.

It is common where suitable habitats are available. During the 1960s it showed a tendency towards the colonisation of drier habitats but recently numbers may have declined and reversed that trend.

COOT *Fulica atra*
Resident and winter visitor.

It breeds fairly commonly on all the larger waters and gravel pits with suitable cover. It can also be found on the wider, more gently flowing stretches of the larger rivers. Occasionally it breeds on smaller ponds and sewage farms with permanent open water and bred on the By Brook during 1978.

Numbers increase considerably during the late autumn particularly in the Cotswold Water Park; these winter visitors presumably originate in central Europe.

GREAT BUSTARD *Otis tarda*
Former resident.

It formerly bred on Salisbury Plain and the Marlborough Downs. It is doubtful if it was ever very common and it certainly decreased as more efficient farming methods were introduced. Unfortunately for the bustard it was large and palatable and the inaugural feast of the Mayors of Salisbury had roast bustard as the main dish.

By 1534 its eggs were protected by law and an Act of 1775 provided for a close season. The latter legislation was rather too late as the bustard was becoming scarce by 1785 and by 1800 was decidedly rare. The last known breeding record was that of a flightless immature being ridden down and captured near Broad Hinton in 1806.

There were a few other records during the last century including one near Stonehenge and one shot in Savernake Forest in 1849. Of a flock of seven which visited the county in January 1871, one was shot at Maddington and another at Berwick St. James. One was shot near Salisbury in January 1880, a winter when several were reported in the country and a female was shot near Chippenham in February 1891, one of eight seen during that winter in England and Wales.

In an attempt to reintroduce the species a small flock has been released into a large enclosure at Porton Down. At the time of writing breeding has not taken place.

STONE CURLEW *Burhinus oedicnemus*

Summer visitor.

It has apparently decreased this century probably due to the 'improvement' of downland pastures, the reduction in the rabbit population since myxomatosis in the 1950s and the increase in cereal growing. Birds whose traditional nest sites were associated with the chalk rubble around warrens have been forced on to cultivated land which provides a similar habitat but which has to be worked several times during the nesting season. Breeding still takes place on Salisbury Plain, Porton Down and in the south and south-west and possibly on the Marlborough Downs. Since 1975 there has been a slight increase in the number of sight records which perhaps indicates a real increase in numbers. During the last three years there have been ten to eighteen pairs occupying breeding sites and it is doubtful if more than one or two pairs remained unlocated.

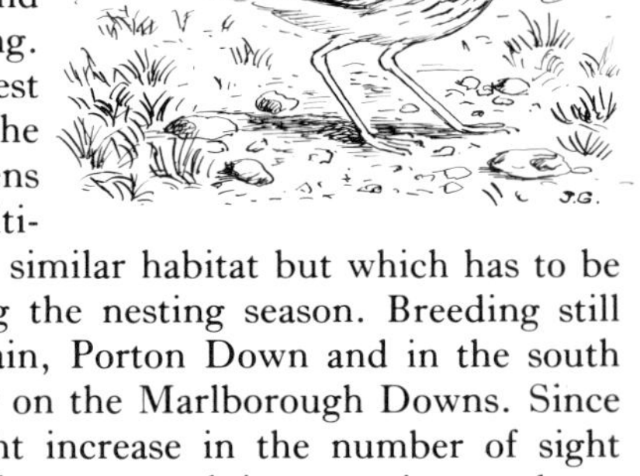

It normally arrives in March and departs in October but there are a few records indicating that it may occasionally overwinter. An individual ringed at Porton in July 1973 was recovered in southern France in September 1974.

LITTLE RINGED PLOVER *Charadrius dubius*

Summer visitor.

The first records for the county were during 1959, at Ashton Keynes in April and at Coate Water in August. At about this time the species was colonising the gravel pits in south Gloucestershire. Other records prior to its establishment as a breeding visitor were as follows: a single bird at Coate Water in April 1960 and in August 1962; singles at Swindon sewage farm in September 1963 and July 1965; two adults at the same site in August 1965 and two juveniles there in August 1967. From 1969 it became a regular autumn visitor to the sewage farm and a pair summered at a site in the north of the county.

Breeding was proved in 1970 when three young were known to have been reared on a gravel pit where two pairs had laid eggs. Various gravel pit sites have been occupied ever since 1970 with the maximum number of pairs in any one year being five. Eggs were laid at Coate Water in 1976 but these failed to hatch. Two other sites away from the main breeding areas have been sporadically occupied without breeding being proved. The continued presence of this species as a breeding bird is greatly dependent upon the availability of gravel pits providing the right habitat. It is of interest to note that two pairs bred on partially flooded plough near Steeple Langford during 1980. Thanks to the generous cooperation of the farmer concerned, both pairs reared young.

It normally arrives in late March or early April and departs in September. The earliest recorded date in spring was 22nd March 1970 and the latest date of departure was 28th September 1975.

LAPWING *Vanellus vanellus*

Resident.

It breeds commonly throughout the county but appears to have marked habitat preferences and some apparently suitable areas are not utilised. The breeding grounds, the majority of which are on cultivated land, are occupied from late February until July and fresh clutches may be found well into June. As the species is apparently single-brooded a great number of replacement clutches must be laid. This ability must have a bearing on the fact that there has been no significant change in status during the present century.

Large flocks numbering 2,000/3,000 are formed in autumn and winter, these also resorting to traditional sites. Flocking normally commences in July when the birds tend to congregate in wetter and open areas to complete their moult. High open downland is largely deserted in winter but some sheltered valleys, such as the Pewsey Vale, support birds throughout the year. During the periods of severe winter weather the flocks tend to fragment with many birds moving on and the remainder moving to the lower ground of river valleys and smaller enclosed fields, favoured areas being around Wroughton and in the Salisbury Avon valley. Occasionally large flocks can be seen overflying to the west and south-west. Some of the flocks presumably contain migrants but there appears to be only one record of a foreign ringed bird occurring in the county. A bird ringed at Hoyland, Rogaland, Norway in May 1951 was recovered at Malmesbury in April 1952. A bird ringed as a chick at Old Sarum in May 1959 was shot near Madrid in January 1963, and another ringed at High Post in June 1969 was killed in south-west France in December 1971.

All the 10 km. squares contain breeding birds but distribution is very uneven and density varies considerably.

SNIPE *Gallinago gallinago*

Resident and winter visitor.

Apparently it did not breed in the last century and there is no accurate information to indicate when breeding first took place. Certainly a few pairs bred in the valleys of the Kennet, and the Salisbury and Bristol Avons during the 1930s. At present breeding takes place in wet meadows along the Kennet from Marlborough to Chilton Foliat. Only a few pairs are involved, not exceeding ten in recent years. Display has been noted in the valleys of the Bourne, Salisbury Avon, Wylye and Nadder but very few nests have been found in the last ten years. A few pairs, less than four in the past three years, still attempt to breed in the Thames valley around Inglesham. There are no recent breeding records for the Bristol Avon. The total number of breeding pairs in 1978 did not exceed 20.

During the autumn and winter numbers increase and a few sites, notably Britford water meadows and Swindon sewage farm, may hold loose flocks of up to 100. One bird ringed at Britford in January 1962 was shot in W. Flanders the following October.

WOODCOCK *Scolopax rusticola*

Resident and winter visitor.

There would appear to be little or no difference in the current distribution from that determined by the 1934/35 enquiry (Alexander).

Breeding has taken place recently at Bentley Wood, Bedwyn Common, Blackmoor Copse, Grovely Wood, Longleat, Savernake, Angrove and Somerford Common. It probably still breeds at the following sites where roding is regularly observed: Ashley Copse, Collingbourne Woods, Corsham Court,

Longley Wood, Webbs Wood and Yarnbrook. It is doubtful if more than 50 pairs breed at the regularly occupied sites.

It is more widespread in winter when it may be found in quite small woods and damp lowland scrub, but numbers vary considerably.

CURLEW *Numenius arquata*
Summer visitor.

There is a record of a week-old chick being killed by a dog near Tidworth in 1916 which would seem to be the first breeding record.

During 1946 a nest was discovered near West Lavington and in subsequent years further nests were found in the same general area, from Pewsey in the east to the Devizes/West Lavington road in the west. Recently numbers in this area appear to have decreased, probably because many of the damp meadows have been drained and reseeded. In the early 1950s breeding took place at Sandridge Park, Etchilhampton, Seend Cleeve and Ogbourne St. George, when pairs were also noted at Bulkington and Keevil, breeding probably taking place at the former. In 1954 pairs were reported north of Chippenham and at Semley, Littlecote and Wroughton. During 1955 pairs were located west of Swindon and at Blunsdon, the latter site being occupied continuously to 1978. Nests were found at Walcot (Swindon), Wanborough and Bishopstone (Swindon) in 1958 and both the latter sites were still in use in 1978. A pair attempted to breed at Coate Water in 1960 and there were four pairs at Inglesham in 1961 and one present there in 1978. A single pair bred at Bincknoll in 1966 with two pairs annually into the mid-1970s. Since 1967 several pairs have bred in the Red Lodge Wood/Somerford Common/Braydon Pond triangle with at least six pairs in 1978. A nest was found near Red Lodge Wood in 1968 containing seven eggs, all apparently laid by the same female.

The areas used for breeding in the county are all similar, damp meadows cut for hay and well provided with marshy patches. The breeding population is rather unstable and site fidelity is low, new sites being occupied for a few years and then deserted. The total numbers of pairs in the county in 1978 was 14 or 15 and three nests were found.

REDSHANK *Tringa totanus*
Summer visitor.

Smith listed only two records for the last century. It now breeds regularly within the county, but only small numbers.

The earliest known breeding record was at Downton in 1907 followed by one at Stitchcombe in 1920. By 1940 it was breeding in all the major river valleys and by 1960 at Ogbourne St. Andrew, Coate Water and Ashton Keynes. There was an almost complete absence of breeding pairs after the severe winter of 1962/63 when the majority of breeding sites were deserted. Since 1964 numbers have steadily increased and most of the original sites were reoccupied by 1970. During 1978 breeding took place at Coate Water, Inglesham, Chilton Foliat and Ashton Keynes. Pairs were seen at other sites along the valleys of the Kennet, the Bourne, the Salisbury Avon and its southerly tributaries. Between 40 and 50 pairs have been present during the summers of 1976/77/78.

COMMON SANDPIPER *Actitis hypoleucos*
Passage migrant, has bred.

A regular and often common migrant. Spring passage during April, early May and autumn passage from July to October. There are a few records of birds summering and wintering, usually only one or two individuals being involved in any one year.

The only breeding record is that of a single adult seen with two chicks near Steeple Langford during 1980.

COMMON TERN *Sterna hirundo*
Passage migrant, has bred.

Until recently many of the "sea terns" seen in the county were not specifically identified. Modern identification techniques have enabled far more to be correctly assigned, thus reducing the numbers of those labelled "commic". This species is a regular spring and autumn passage migrant in small numbers, most frequently seen at Coate Water, Corsham Lake and in the Water Park. In both 1979 and 1980 a pair reared young on an island in a gravel pit near Ashton Keynes.

STOCK DOVE *Columba oenas*
Resident.

Common and widely distributed, breeding throughout the county and where natural sites are not available it nests in buildings and other man-made structures including army target vehicles. Whilst most commonly seen in pairs or small parties it does occasionally form very large flocks.

WOODPIGEON *Columba palumbus*
Resident.

It is very common and widely distributed, breeding in large numbers in all areas. In recent years it has increased and now breeds in gardens in the centres of the largest towns. It forms vast flocks in winter when numbers are probably augmented by immigrants.

COLLARED DOVE *Streptopelia decaocto*
Resident.

It was first noted at Marlborough in May 1962 where three birds were seen, apparently two males and a female and two young were reared from a nest in a garden in the centre of the town. In 1963 single birds were seen at Devizes and Pitton and up to five at Amesbury, and by the end of that year the Marlborough population had risen to 17 individuals. There were at least twenty pairs in Marlborough during 1964 and most of the villages around the town had been colonised. Birds were also seen at Ramsbury and most of the villages around Salisbury. By 1965 Chippenham and the area to the south, east and west of the town reported a sprinkling of single birds and the first colonists arrived in Salisbury, Landford and Clarendon. Breeding took place in Swindon during 1966 and the spread continued in Salisbury and through the central villages of the Avon and the Bourne. During 1967 breeding occurred at Malmesbury and large flocks were building up in some of the areas colonised earlier. At this time the only notable gaps in the species' distribution were in the Warminster, Westbury and Trowbridge areas where breeding was proved by 1970.

The rapid increase and subsequent build-up of large autumn flocks caused some concern amongst farmers particularly those who grew and processed cereal crops. In some places the species is regarded as a pest, although autumn flocks have tended to decrease in the past three or four years.

TURTLE DOVE *Streptopelia turtur*

Summer visitor.

A fairly common summer visitor normally arriving in late April or early May. It breeds in all the 10 km. squares but is rather local in some areas, tending to be most numerous on arable farmland and the rough grassland of the Plain. It normally departs in September with stragglers into October. Extreme arrival and departure dates are 25th March 1970 and 21st October 1950.

CUCKOO *Cuculus canorus*

Summer visitor.

Recent reports are rather conflicting, some indicating an increase and others a decrease. There is little doubt that there has been a decrease during the past 20 years but this may have slowed down recently.

Breeding occurs in all the 10 km. squares although sparsely on high arable land. Host species noted include Meadow Pipit, Tree Pipit, Dunnock, Pied Wagtail, Robin, Reed Warbler and Reed Bunting – listed in descending order of frequency of being parasitised.

It normally arrives in April with adults departing in July and early August and juveniles in August and September. Extreme arrival and departure dates are 26th March 1968 and 2nd December 1916.

BARN OWL *Tyto alba*
Resident.

It was formerly common but numbers are now very much reduced. The major reason for the decline appears to have been the indiscriminate use of rat poisons and crop pesticides. The severe winter of 1962/63 added further casualties from which recovery has been very slow. Another hazard is the species' apparent susceptibility to collision with fast moving road vehicles.

LITTLE OWL *Athene noctua*
Resident, introduced.

There were very few records for the last century and their origins were not determined. The first, presumably an introduced bird, was shot at Amesbury in 1907.

The species began to colonise the county from the south-east in about 1911 and bred at Downton in 1915. By 1920 it was distributed quite widely (*British Birds* 1x, 21.). Numbers seem to remain fairly steady and breeding has been proved in 27 of the 10 km. squares. Nest sites include rabbit holes on the downs in the south.

TAWNY OWL *Strix aluco*
Resident.

It is common and widespread, breeding in all the 10 km. squares. The species is tolerant of a wide range of habitats and breeds in marginal areas not inhabited by other owls.

LONG-EARED OWL *Asio otus*

Resident.

Formerly common in some areas, it is now a rare resident found only in a few scattered localities. A cause of its decline may be competition with the Tawny Owl. The latter species appears to drive out, and may even kill, the former.

It breeds sparingly in downland conifer plantations, shelter belts and rarely in juniper and hawthorn scrub. It is probably a regular winter visitor in small numbers to rough downland scrub similar to that frequented by *A. flammeus*. In this habitat it may be confused with the latter and consequently is under-recorded.

SHORT-EARED OWL *Asio flammeus*

Winter visitor, has bred.

A winter visitor seen in most years but in variable numbers. Favourite wintering sites include rough grassland and scrub on the Marlborough Downs and Salisbury Plain. It normally arrives in October and departs in April.

There are fairly frequent late spring and early summer records but the only reliable breeding record was of a pair which reared young near Snail Down in 1964. Another pair apparently attempted to breed on the ranges in 1967. The birds were present throughout the summer but the nest was not found nor were young seen.

NIGHTJAR *Caprimulgus europaeus*

Summer visitor.

It was formerly not uncommon but has decreased greatly in recent years and is now known to breed only in Bentley Wood,

Grovely Wood, Longleat, Porton Down and possibly at Bulford, all sites in the northern half of the county having been vacated. Extreme arrival and departure dates are 5th April 1968 and 20th October 1978.

SWIFT *Apus apus*
Summer visitor.

A common summer visitor breeding in all the 10 km. squares. A little less common in the centre of some of the larger towns than it used to be due to the modernisation of older areas and the subsequent loss of breeding sites. Normally it arrives in late April, departing in August and early September. Extreme dates are 4th April 1956 and 11th October 1978.

KINGFISHER *Alcedo atthis*
Resident.

A relatively common resident whose population tends to fluctuate. Hard winters can cause serious mortality but losses tend to be quickly replaced. Before the severe winter of 1978/79 most suitable breeding areas appeared to be occupied with numbers at a high level but first reports for 1979 indicate a high winter mortality with the majority of breeding sites subsequently unoccupied.

It breeds more commonly on the less polluted Salisbury Avon and its tributaries than on the Kennet, Bristol Avon, Thames, By Brook, Ray, Cole and the Kennet and Avon Canal. Most of the larger waters have occasional pairs including gravel pits in the Ashton Keynes section of the Cotswold Water Park.

HOOPOE *Upupa epops*

Rare summer visitor.

A rare visitor in the last century although there is evidence to suggest that breeding took place at Rodbourne Cheney and Stratford-sub-Castle. During this century records have been more frequent, these being mainly in spring but also in summer and autumn. There are breeding records for central areas in 1948, 1950, 1955 and 1971 although some of these are not too well documented.

WRYNECK *Jynx torquilla*

Former summer visitor.

Formerly a common summer visitor which was already decreasing towards the end of the nineteenth century. Breeding became sporadic early this century and by 1920 the species had become rare even on passage. The last known nest was at West Dean in 1950, since when there have been no records during the breeding season.

Individuals are regularly seen on autumn passage, numbers fluctuating from year to year, but it is now seldom seen in spring.

GREEN WOODPECKER *Picus viridis*

Resident.

It was a common resident in the past but is much less common now. The severe winter of 1947 caused heavy mortality throughout the county and recovery was very slow.

Recolonisation of traditional sites had hardly been completed when the cold winter of 1962/63 reduced the population once more. Recovery has again been slow and in 1978 some areas still remained unoccupied. At present the majority of typical habitats, such as woodland adjacent to unploughed downland where active anthills are present, are well populated but low lying farmland supports fewer pairs than previously.

GREAT SPOTTED WOODPECKER *Dendrocopos major*
Resident.

Considered to be the least common of the woodpeckers in the last century, it is now widely distributed and by far the commonest of the three.

In 1947 there was a marked decrease but numbers rose fairly quickly to approximately the same level within a few years. During the 1962/63 severe winter there was heavy mortality but recovery was again quite rapid, far quicker than that of the preceding species. At present it is widely distributed and common in some areas, breeding in all the 10 km. squares.

Since 1976 there may have been a further increase in numbers. This may have been due to the Dutch elm disease beetle providing extra food and causing a genuine increase or the resulting loss of foliage making the existing birds more visible. During this period there have been instances of the species damaging nest boxes to obtain the nestlings inside, and of similar damage to nests of House Martins.

LESSER SPOTTED WOODPECKER *Dendrocopos minor*
Resident.

It is widely distributed but less common than the other woodpeckers, having a marked preference for mature gardens and parkland with old decaying trees. It often breeds in villages and the outskirts of towns.

The severe winters of early 1947 and 1962/63 caused far less mortality in this species than in the other two woodpeckers. What losses there were seemed to have been quickly replaced. As can be seen from the map, the higher ground tends to be avoided, river valleys and lower ground being more favoured.

WOODLARK *Lullula arborea*
Resident.

At present it is extremely rare and there have been no breeding records since 1963. This species was never very common but bred regularly in those areas bordering the New Forest. Other sites included Bowood, Spye Park and Coate Water where small numbers bred more or less regularly. Breeding has also taken place near Marlborough, Everleigh, Grovely Wood, Longleat, Porton Down and, very rarely, at one or two other sites.

The highest density was around 1950 followed by a steady decrease until the prolonged 1962/63 cold spell apparently exterminated it in the county. There have been a few winter records in each of the past three years but no summering pairs have been located.

SKYLARK *Alauda arvensis*
Resident.

A very common resident particularly in open country and on marginal land such as rough grassland, building sites, allotments and motorway verges. It breeds in all the 10 km. squares within the county. It forms into large flocks in winter when numbers may be augmented by migrants.

SAND MARTIN *Riparia riparia*

Summer visitor.

It is common on both spring and autumn passage but only breeds in any numbers in the north of the county. Small transient colonies can be found in river banks and artificial sites, such as drainage holes in walls and banks including earthenware pipes, have been used. Larger colonies occur in the Cotswold Water Park and at the sand pits at Calne. One bird ringed at Calne in August 1968 was recovered in Algeria at the end of May 1969.

Early arrivals can be found in March but the majority arrive in early April. Breeding sites are deserted in early September and autumn passage is usually over by the middle of that month. The earliest arrival date is 4th March 1977 and the latest departure date 8th October 1966.

SWALLOW *Hirundo rustica*

Summer visitor.

A common summer visitor breeding widely throughout the county. The decrease this century has apparently accelerated in recent years.

Peirson suggested that the autumn migration routes are from east to west across the county. There is some strong supporting evidence which shows that this species and the House Martin tend to follow the line of the high northward facing escarpments. The escarpments of both the Marlborough Downs and the Plain have a generally south-westwards inclination from the east. Birds ringed as chicks in the county have been recovered in France (two) and in South Africa, and a bird ringed in Belgium in May 1965 was found nesting at Woodford in June 1966.

It normally arrives early in April with the majority arriving in the second half of the month. March records are not uncommon, the earliest being 18th March 1968. Autumn passage is protracted, beginning in August and continuing into October, the latest autumn date being 2nd December 1957.

HOUSE MARTIN *Delichon urbica*

Summer visitor.

A common summer visitor, widespread within the limits imposed by its breeding requirements. Numbers have decreased in recent years but evidence is difficult to obtain due to the bird's habit of deserting nest sites after a few years and moving to new ones, but in 1978 they were lower than usual, many sites being deserted and few new ones being located.

Generally it arrives in April towards the end of the month but often not in numbers until early May; and departs in late September and October with stragglers into November, the earliest and latest dates being 5th March 1967 and 3rd December 1959 respectively.

TREE PIPIT *Anthus trivialis*

Summer visitor.

A widely distributed summer visitor breeding in most of the larger, wooded areas and in downland scrub where there are scattered large bushes and small trees. About 30 pairs breed north of the Kennet and east of the Bristol Avon and approximately double this number breed in and around Savernake Forest, West Woods and the surrounding downland. Numbers for other areas are unknown.

It normally arrives in April, departing in late August and early September. Extreme dates are 1st April 1970 and 11th October 1953.

MEADOW PIPIT *Anthus pratensis*

Summer and winter visitor.

It breeds on sheltered downland slopes, commonly in a few areas and less regularly on rough lowland sites. Recently it has bred on derelict factory sites in central Swindon.

A common winter visitor widespread throughout the county,

roosting in long grass on downland such as Oliver's Castle, although most breeding sites tend to be deserted at this time. Local breeding birds may well be nomadic or only summer visitors to their breeding localities.

Large numbers pass through on both spring and autumn passage. Migration watches along the chalk escarpments have shown that this species appears to ignore topographical features when on migration.

YELLOW WAGTAIL *Motacilla flava*
Summer visitor.

A local summer visitor to low lying and wetter parts of the county. It breeds in small numbers in the valleys of the Salisbury Avon and its tributaries, also along the Kennet and the upper Bristol Avon. There are a few scattered breeding records for the Avon around Chippenham. The greatest breeding density is in the Thames valley particularly around Swindon, Cricklade and Ashton Keynes. Although estimates vary it is doubtful if more than 150 pairs breed in the county in any one year. Autumn roosts have been reported from Ashton Keynes, Coate Water, Corsham Lake, Lacock and Stanton Fitzwarren. One bird ringed at Coate Water in September 1962 was found dead on the beach near Santander, Spain the following April.

Individuals showing characteristics of the race *Motacilla f. flava* have been seen in most recent springs and occasionally in earlier years. Breeding of these variants took place in both 1907 and 1909 and pairs summered at Coate Water in 1976, '77 and '78.

It normally arrives in April and departs from late August into September. Extreme dates are 20th March 1969 and 13th December 1970.

GREY WAGTAIL *Motacilla cinerea*
Resident and winter visitor.

There is little information regarding this species from the last century but it would seem to have been uncommon.

During this century the number of breeding pairs increased until the severe winter of 1962/63 when there was a catastrophic decrease. In the spring of 1963 it was found that the majority of breeding sites were deserted but recovery was relatively rapid and numbers had risen to pre-1962 levels by 1969. During 1971 a survey was carried out in the county in an attempt to determine the breeding population. A total of 129 pairs were located of which 76 were proved to have bred (Tyler and Tyler, W.A.M. 67). It was discovered that the slow-flowing muddier rivers, Thames, Ray, Cole and the lower Bristol Avon, had few pairs but the faster-flowing chalk streams and the limestone By Brook were well populated, the latter with a mean distance between pairs of less than a mile (1.6 km.). Suitable nest sites would appear to have been a limiting factor on the faster shallower rivers and lack of feeding areas on the deeper rivers of the north.

Since the survey there has been a further increase particularly in the north where breeding has taken place at sites well away from rivers and at some of the larger areas of open water. Assuming that the situation on the faster flowing rivers has remained unaltered, the 1978 breeding population was c. 150 pairs.

PIED WAGTAIL *Motacilla alba*
Resident.

A fairly common resident breeding in all the 10 km. squares. It is less common on higher more exposed downland which is largely deserted in winter.

The town centres of Bradford-on-Avon, Chippenham, Calne, Devizes, Trowbridge, Salisbury and Swindon have roosts in trees or on buildings and there is a large assembly at the British Leyland factory in Swindon.

Birds of the nominate race *M. a. alba* are regularly identified in spring and occasionally in autumn.

Two birds ringed in the county have been recovered in western France.

DIPPER *Cinclus cinclus*
Resident.

A scarce resident not known to breed until 1897 when a nest was found at Castle Combe. The By Brook was slowly colonised and from 1910 a slow expansion began southwards down the western side of the county. During the last ten years breeding has taken place on the By Brook (up to four pairs), Cole (one pair), Fonthill Lake (one pair), Wylye (two pairs), Ebble (one pair), Nadder (one pair), Biss Brook (one pair) and near Chippenham (one pair). Pairs and single birds have also been seen on the Kennet, Bristol Avon, Thames and at Coate Water and Wardour Lake.

Numbers fluctuate slightly but sight records at new sites have tended to increase in the recent past.

WREN *Troglodytes troglodytes*
Resident.

A common and widespread resident which is susceptible to cold winters and was almost wiped out by that of 1962/63. Numbers were quickly made up and by 1974/75 the species had attained its highest ever density but early reports for 1979 suggest that severe weather in the first months of that year resulted in another drop in the population. It breeds in all the 10 km. squares.

DUNNOCK *Prunella modularis*
Resident.

A very common resident breeding throughout the county,

except in the large blocks of grassland on the Salisbury Plain military training areas, where no suitable habitats are available.

ROBIN *Erithacus rubecula*
Resident.

A very common and widespread breeding resident, except in military training areas as for the previous species.

NIGHTINGALE *Luscinia megarhynchos*
Summer visitor.

Although it breeds throughout the county it is nowhere common and is infrequent on high ground. A recent survey, which was far from complete, recorded a total of 172 singing males of which only 15 were above 500 feet (152 m.).

There was an apparent increase in numbers after the last war but this gain had apparently been lost by 1960. Several traditional sites in the north of the county remained unoccupied until 1980. That year saw the re-occupation of many sites with numbers at their highest for some thirty years.

It normally arrives in mid April departing in August. Extreme arrival and departure dates are 10th March 1961 and 30th August 1970.

BLACK REDSTART *Phoenicurus ochruros*
Passage migrant, has bred.

Mainly a late autumn visitor in very small numbers, occasionally seen in late spring and during the winter. It was a very rare visitor in the last century and during the first 30 years of the present one.

A pair reared two broods at Bulford in both 1975 and 1976. The female returned in 1977 and laid a clutch of infertile eggs. A female was seen at Netheravon in August 1976 accompanied by two juveniles. A pair reared ten young in Swindon in 1979, the nest sites being in a factory building in continual use. Breeding had been suspected in the area in previous years but without confirmation.

REDSTART *Phoenicurus phoenicurus*

Summer visitor.

An uncommon summer visitor breeding sparingly in old woods and parkland. Formerly it was not uncommon but numbers began to decrease early in the present century. In spite of continuing changes in the habitat and disturbance by military activities, one or two pairs still breed in Imber village. (This demonstrates remarkable fidelity by the species to a particular site.) On passage it is more often seen in autumn than in spring but numbers fluctuate widely from year to year. The earliest recorded date is 15th March 1975 and the latest 7th November 1963.

WHINCHAT *Saxicola rubetra*

Summer visitor.

Apparently it was a common visitor in the last century and is certainly much less numerous now although it still breeds in most of the areas with suitable habitats. The majority of breeding records are for the Imber, Everleigh and Larkhill military training areas. It breeds regularly on the Marlborough Downs from Fyfield in the west to the county boundary in the east, seldom more than eight pairs having been recorded. Isolated pairs breed in other areas particularly in the south-east. It is doubtful if more than 50 pairs have bred in Wiltshire in any of the last five years.

It normally arrives in April, the earliest date being 5th April 1959, and departs in September, the latest date being 28th November 1971.

STONECHAT *Saxicola torquata*
Resident and summer visitor.

At the beginning of the century it was still a reasonably common resident having been quite numerous in the nineteenth century, but during most of this century it has been an uncommon breeding summer visitor with an increase in numbers in the late autumn. During the last ten years, however, there has been an increase in the number of breeding pairs. Since 1974 breeding has taken place on Imber Ranges (up to 3 pairs), Porton Down (2 pairs), Greenland Camp (1 pair), Grovely Wood (1 pair), Haxton Down (1 pair) and single pairs may well have bred at Everleigh and at another site in the extreme south of the county. It is doubtful if more than 12 pairs have bred in the county in any year since the last war.

Birds overwinter both in breeding areas and in traditional wintering sites, such as the upper Thames valley around Swindon, in habitats where cover and food are available – as in kale and strip-grazed root crops.

WHEATEAR *Oenanthe oenanthe*
Summer visitor.

Formerly a common summer visitor to upland areas of the county the number of pairs breeding during this century has greatly decreased particularly since the 1940s. The ploughing of downland during the last war caused a reduction in suitable nest sites and confined the remaining pairs to the higher and steeper downs. After the myxomatosis epidemic in 1956 which greatly reduced the rabbit population numbers again declined, probably because of the increasing length of the grass and shortage of nesting holes.

Since 1974 there have been only a very few records of breeding, these being on Imber Ranges, Porton Down, Fyfield Down and at Swindon. The latter concerned a pair attempting to breed on a derelict factory site in the centre of the town. It is unlikely that more than six pairs have attempted to breed in any one year since 1974.

Small parties are regularly seen on passage at former downland breeding sites. It usually arrives in March and early April, the earliest date being 17th February 1965, and departs in September and October, the latest recorded on 18th November 1960.

BLACKBIRD *Turdus merula*

Resident.

It is very common, breeding throughout the county. Numbers are augmented in late autumn by migrants, presumably from western and northern Europe. A bird ringed in Amsterdam in September 1959 was found dead at Little Durnford in January 1960; one ringed at Cole Park in March 1973 was recovered in West Germany in September 1977; another ringed in Finland in March 1971 was recovered at Malmesbury in January 1976.

SONG THRUSH *Turdus philomelos*

Resident.

It is a very common breeding resident, although much less numerous than the Blackbird. The population has yet to recover from the 1962/63 winter which caused heavy mortality, and the dry summers of 1975 and 1976 reduced the number of young reared. As with the Blackbird, numbers rise during the autumn due to migrants although most of these appear to be transient.

One ringed in Germany in May 1960 was recovered at Calne in April 1962.

MISTLE THRUSH *Turdus viscivorus*

Resident.

A common breeding resident, widespread throughout the county but much less numerous than either Blackbird or Song Thrush due to its larger territorial requirement and the presence of large areas from which its preferred habitat is absent but which can support populations of the other two species.

It forms nomadic flocks in late summer which rarely exceed 100 individuals and are usually much smaller. By late autumn many adults are back in their breeding territories and song can be heard regularly from November.

GRASSHOPPER WARBLER *Locustella naevia*

Summer visitor.

It is a regular summer visitor. Numbers fluctuate but it is not usually numerous. During fieldwork for the BTO "Atlas of Breeding Birds" it was proved to have bred in 17 of the 10 km. squares. The distribution tends to vary due to the transient nature of some of its preferred habitats such as young forestry plantations and areas of rank grassland with scattered scrub.

It normally arrives in April, the earliest date recorded is 8th April 1966, departing in August and September with stragglers up to 2nd October.

SEDGE WARBLER *Acrocephalus schoenobaenus*

Summer visitor.

Not uncommon at some localities such as Coate Water, the Kennet and Avon canal, lower Salisbury Avon and in the Cotswold Water Park. It breeds in most damp areas with suitable cover though only in small numbers but it is not entirely confined to low lying marshy sites. In good years it can be found breeding in scrub on high downland, for example it has bred regularly on the Marlborough Downs at heights up to 825 ft. (250 m.).

It normally arrives in April and departs in September, extreme dates being 23rd March 1957 and 23rd October 1952. A bird ringed at Coate Water in September 1967 was recovered at Heligoland, Germany in May 1968 and one ringed at Corsham Lake was recovered in Pyrénées-Atlantiques, France.

MARSH WARBLER *Acrocephalus palustris*
Summer visitor.

An uncommon summer visitor breeding only sporadically until recently. During the last four years one site has been occupied by a breeding pair, which reared young in 1977 and 1980. A singing male was located at another site in the summer of 1978.

REED WARBLER *Acrocephalus scirpaceus*
Summer visitor.

A regular summer visitor to the few sites in the county where it breeds. Up to 40 pairs can be found in the *Phragmites* beds at Coate Water, c. 12 pairs at Corsham Lake, c. 8 pairs at Stanton Fitzwarren, c. 15 pairs in the Cotswold Water Park, c. 12 pairs at Westbury Ponds and c. 20 pairs in the reed beds of the upper Salisbury Avon valley. An unknown number breed to the south of Salisbury and a few pairs along deep *Phragmites*-fringed ditches in the north and along the banks of the Kennet and Avon canal.

It normally arrives late in April or early May, departing in September. The earliest and latest dates are 3rd April 1958 and 16th October 1975. Birds ringed at Coate Water have been recovered in France and Spain.

DARTFORD WARBLER *Sylvia undata*

Resident.

Previously a not uncommon resident breeding on gorse-covered downs. The majority of these sites have disappeared except for a small area in the extreme south. During this century numbers have decreased to the point where only one or two pairs have been breeding along the county boundary but it is doubtful if they have bred since 1976.

Very occasionally individuals are seen in autumn and winter at sites outside the breeding areas.

LESSER WHITETHROAT *Sylvia curruca*

Summer visitor.

A fairly common summer visitor but numbers fluctuate widely from year to year. It breeds in all the 10 km. squares, apparently being commoner in the thick hedgerows of the north and west of the county. Higher ground tends to be avoided except on passage.

It usually arrives in late

April or early May departing in late August and September, extreme dates being 3rd April 1957 and 27th September 1976.

WHITETHROAT *Sylvia communis*
Summer visitor.

A very common summer visitor until 1969 when there was a catastrophic decrease. This decrease was apparently due to adverse conditions in the wintering range in central Africa. Recovery has been very slow. For a number of years males have outnumbered females with the result that almost continuous song was heard from males failing to attract mates. Since 1975 numbers have slowly increased but the population is still only a fraction of that prior to 1969.

One ringed at Idmiston in July 1963 was recovered in Spain in October of the same year.

Extreme arrival and departure dates are 31st March 1958 and 4th November 1976.

GARDEN WARBLER *Sylvia borin*
Summer visitor.

It is widely distributed throughout the county but much less common than the Blackcap. Requiring thicker and more extensive cover than that species, this preference tends to limit its frequency. It breeds in all the 10 km. squares, sparingly on high ground but commonly in low lying woodland. One ringed at Marlborough in June 1962 was recovered in Morocco in May 1965.

It normally arrives in early May and departs in September. The earliest date is 31st March 1956 and the latest 2nd October 1965.

BLACKCAP *Sylvia atricapilla*
Summer and winter visitor.

A common and well distributed summer visitor even breeding on the higher hills where suitable cover is available. In recent years it has shown an increasing tendency to overwinter particularly in more sheltered districts. It is fond of suburban gardens with well stocked bird tables and berry-bearing shrubs.

The normal arrival and departure times have become obscured

due to the number of wintering birds.

One ringed at Coate Water in August 1964 was recovered in western France in October 1964 and another ringed at Chippenham in July 1967 was recovered in Spain in October 1967.

WOOD WARBLER *Phylloscopus sibilatrix*

Summer visitor.

A decreasing summer visitor breeding in very small numbers in some of the beech woods on the chalk. A small number of pairs probably still breeds in the extreme south and south-west of the county. There were at least six pairs in woodland near Marlborough in 1980. It is infrequently seen in other areas on passage.

It usually arrives in late April and departs in August and early September; the earliest spring date is 24th March 1948 and the latest autumn date 17th September 1952.

CHIFFCHAFF *Phylloscopus collybita*

Summer visitor.

A common summer visitor which breeds throughout the county wherever suitable habitats are available.

Occasionally it overwinters but only in very small numbers, seldom more than one or two in any one winter. Normally it arrives in late March and early April, departing in September with stragglers into October.

Very occasionally individuals of the northern race *P. c. abietinus* have been identified. Birds ringed in Swindon have been recovered in Spain.

WILLOW WARBLER *Phylloscopus trochilus*

Summer visitor.

A very common breeding summer visitor which normally arrives in early to mid-April and departs in August and September. Extreme dates are 5th March 1959 and 27th September 1976. One bird ringed at Marlborough was recovered in Spain.

An individual of the race *P. t. acredula* was identified at Pitton in 1949.

GOLDCREST *Regulus regulus*

Resident.

At present it is a common and widespread breeding resident. Numbers can crash dramatically during severe winters and those of 1916/17, 1946/47 and 1962/63 almost exterminated it in Wiltshire. Recovery after 1962/63 was comparatively quick and by 1970 the species was at its greatest density this century. This recovery was followed by a slight decrease, mainly in marginal habitats such as downland scrub, small copses and unmanaged hedgerows, a marked decrease in 1979 following severe weather in the early months of that year.

SPOTTED FLYCATCHER *Muscicapa striata*

Summer visitor.

A widespread summer visitor, common in some localities, which breeds in all the 10 km. squares. The number of breeding birds fluctuates considerably from year to year and has probably decreased in the last ten years. One ringed at Chippenham was recovered in Spain.

It usually arrives in late April and early May, the earliest date being 9th April 1949. It departs in September with stragglers into October, the latest on 27th October 1972.

LONG-TAILED TIT *Aegithalos caudatus*

Resident.

A common resident which is liable to heavy losses in prolonged cold winters. At present there is a large and widespread population breeding in all the 10 km. squares.

MARSH TIT *Parus palustris*

Resident.

A common resident most frequently occurring in low-lying woodland and rather scarce on high ground. Although reported from all the 10 km. squares there are three squares in which breeding has not been proved.

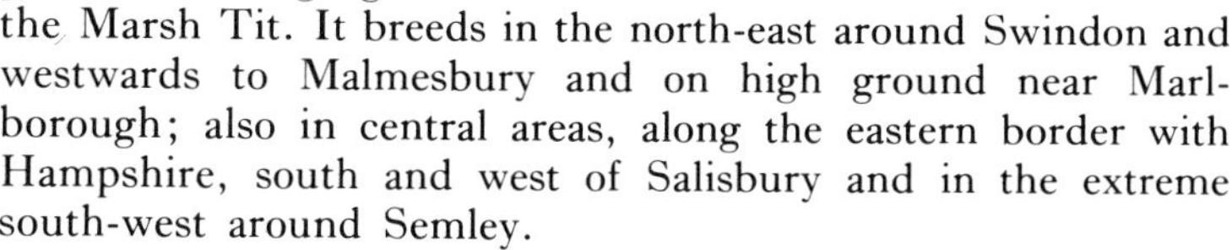

WILLOW TIT *Parus montanus*

Resident.

An uncommon resident which is more frequently reported from high ground than the Marsh Tit. It breeds in the north-east around Swindon and westwards to Malmesbury and on high ground near Marlborough; also in central areas, along the eastern border with Hampshire, south and west of Salisbury and in the extreme south-west around Semley.

Unfortunately there is still some confusion between this species and the Marsh Tit which tends to obscure the status of each.

COAL TIT *Parus ater*
Resident.

It is a common resident in conifer woodland but less frequent elsewhere. It has been recorded in all the 10 km. squares and breeds in all but one.

BLUE TIT *Parus caeruleus*
Resident.

It is common and widespread throughout the county. Individuals showing characters of the race *P. c. caeruleus* have been trapped in winter.

GREAT TIT *Parus major*
Resident.

It is common and widespread throughout the county.

NUTHATCH *Sitta europaea*
Resident.

It is much less common than formerly and is steadily becoming rarer in the north but it is still breeding in all the 10 km. squares.

TREECREEPER *Certhia familiaris*
Resident.

It is widespread but nowhere common, breeding in 25 of the 10 km. squares. It can be badly affected by severe winters and was almost exterminated in the north of the county by the cold weather in early 1979. Fortunately a rapid recovery has been made with numbers nearly normal in 1980.

RED-BACKED SHRIKE *Lanius collurio*
Summer visitor.

Formerly a common summer visitor, which has been decreasing throughout this century. This decrease accelerated during the period 1950/55 and by 1958 there were only c. 20 pairs remaining. In 1960 only four pairs could be located. There were no records for 1963/64 but two pairs were breeding in a central area during 1966. From 1967 to 1969 a single pair bred at the same central site each year and in 1970 a pair bred in the north. There were no further breeding records until 1977 when a pair was located at Swindon and a nest was found containing three eggs. There was a male near this site in 1978 but no female or nest was seen. During the past 20 years sight records have greatly decreased as in other southern counties.

JAY *Garrulus glandarius*
Resident.

Common in suitably wooded districts and it also occurs less commonly in scrub and thinly wooded areas. It breeds in all the 10 km. squares. Birds presumed to be migrants have been seen moving westwards in small flocks during the autumn.

MAGPIE *Pica pica*
Resident.

A common resident whose numbers are increasing. It has recently moved into the suburbs of the larger towns and breeds in all the 10 km. squares. In some areas numbers are 'regulated' by game preserving interests.

JACKDAW *Corvus monedula*
Resident.

A common breeding resident in well wooded areas and locally common in a very few suburban sites. It has decreased in some of the larger towns, where it was formerly not uncommon. It often forms large flocks during the winter months. Commonly it flocks with Rooks when it tends to be more widespread.

ROOK *Corvus frugilegus*
Resident.

It is a common breeding resident in all the 10 km. squares. The 1975 BTO survey covered all but one square (SU 02) and recorded a total of 25,848 nests. Allowing for omissions due to some counts taking place when rookeries were at less than maximum numbers this would indicate a population of c. 55,000 individuals. A variety of trees were utilised as nest sites with elm the most popular (47%) and beech second (35.7%).

Wiltshire has since lost the majority of its elms, the victims of

Dutch elm disease. In 1978 many nests were being built in dead elms but at several sites pylons carrying high tension cables were used. The nests were built towards the outer ends of the cable-supporting cross members.

CARRION CROW *Corvus corone*

Resident.

A common resident throughout the county breeding in all the 10 km. squares. Numbers appear to increase in winter when large flocks are noted in some areas. The race *C. c. cornix* was formerly a regular winter visitor in small numbers but there have been very few recent records.

RAVEN *Corvus corax*

Vagrant, formerly bred.

During the 19th century it bred in well wooded districts bordering on open country. Since the end of that century it has been an irregular visitor with only twelve records in the past thirty years.

STARLING *Sturnus vulgaris*

Resident and winter visitor.

It is a very common breeding resident. Local birds form small flocks in summer and use communal roosts. Local adults tend to move back into their territories in autumn but the roosts increase in size as the first immigrants arrive. These summer/autumn roosts are largely deserted in winter when vast numbers congregate at the winter roosts.

Birds ringed in the county during the winter months have been recovered in Holland, Germany, Belgium, Poland and Russia.

HOUSE SPARROW *Passer domesticus*

Resident.

A common resident breeding in all the 10 km. squares. They form quite large flocks to feed on cereals in late summer.

TREE SPARROW *Passer montanus*
Resident.

A widespread resident which is more numerous in the north. In some winters fairly large flocks arrive which are presumably winter visitors. These too are more regularly recorded in the north of the county.

CHAFFINCH *Fringilla coelebs*
Resident and winter visitor.

A very common breeding resident throughout the county which often forms quite large flocks in the winter months, when numbers are apparently augmented by migrants. Birds ringed in Norway, Belgium and Holland have been recovered in the county during winter and spring.

GREENFINCH *Carduelis chloris*
Resident.

A common breeding resident in all the 10 km. squares, being more numerous in low lying enclosed areas. It breeds quite commonly in suburbia and sometimes forms large flocks in winter.

GOLDFINCH *Carduelis carduelis*
Resident.

A common and widespread breeding resident which forms

moderately sized flocks in autumn. It would appear to move out of the county in large numbers at this time since winter flocks are generally small and mixed with other finches. Numbers rise again in late March and early April. There are one or two ringing recoveries that suggest that the population is semi-migratory.

LINNET *Carduelis cannabina*
Resident.

It is a common and widespread breeding resident. Its behaviour is similar to that of the Goldfinch in that it flocks in autumn and is then not found in numbers during the winter. It returns in strength normally in late March.

A bird ringed at Porton Down in May was recovered in France in October of the same year and two others have been recovered in Spain.

REDPOLL *Carduelis flammea*
Resident and winter visitor.

It is resident regularly at only one site in the north of the county, at Somerford Common. It has bred irregularly at several localities, the majority of these being north of the Pewsey Vale.

As a winter visitor it occurs in small flocks or ones and twos with other finches when it is found in damp alder or birch woods, kale fields and wet scrub. Birds showing the characteristics of the race *C. f. flammea* have been reported from time to time.

CROSSBILL *Loxia curvirostra*

Resident and irregular visitor.

It has bred irregularly in the south-east of the county since the 1930s and recently was seen carrying nesting material at a site in the south-west. Otherwise it is usually an irregular visitor in late summer or early autumn, most often seen in small parties or singly.

BULLFINCH *Pyrrhula pyrrhula*

Resident.

A common breeding resident in enclosed areas, only occurring on higher ground where thick cover is available.

HAWFINCH *Coccothraustes coccothraustes*

Resident.

Apparently quite common in the middle of the last century, it is now uncommon and seldom reported although it may be overlooked due to its secretive habits.

During fieldwork for the BTO "Atlas of Breeding Birds" it was found breeding in only two squares, both in the south-east and no new records have been reported since.

YELLOWHAMMER *Emberiza citrinella*

Resident.

A common breeding resident in both open and enclosed areas tending to be less common in wetter situations. In the latter localities it is in direct competition with the Reed Bunting but there is no evidence to suggest that either species is losing ground to the other.

It forms flocks in late autumn and winter which occasionally become quite large with up to c. 300 individuals.

CIRL BUNTING *Emberiza cirlus*

Resident.

An uncommon breeding resident now apparently restricted to the south-eastern part of the county, notably the Winterslow area. There used to be a small breeding population around Swindon but no birds have been seen there during the past five years. Other sites in central districts also appear to have been abandoned.

During the early 1970s there was a wintering flock of c. 40 birds near Ford (Salisbury) which may well have contained the majority of the breeding population.

REED BUNTING *Emberiza schoeniclus*

Resident.

A fairly common breeding resident in the wetter areas but it is also found in drier habitats and breeds on high ground where large areas of rank vegetation are available. Since the BTO "Atlas of Breeding Birds" was published in 1976 it has been proved to breed in all the 10 km. squares.

In winter it forms flocks which are usually small but occasionally consist of over one hundred individuals and sometimes contain other buntings and finches. Roosts in reed and osier beds have been reported in several localities, notably Coate Water and Corsham Lake.

CORN BUNTING *Miliaria calandra*

Resident.

A breeding resident, commonest on the chalk uplands of the North Wessex Downs where it breeds in cereal crops and long grass at all altitudes. Its breeding density is apparently partly determined by the presence or absence of fences for use as song posts. It is generally absent from the unfenced military training areas of Salisbury Plain, though in recent years a few males have been recorded singing on hawthorn bushes.

In the Thames valley it breeds near Lechlade, Inglesham, Highworth, South Marston and east of Cricklade. There are other isolated sites in the Bristol Avon catchment area, between Wootton Bassett and Brinkworth and between North Wraxall and Colerne. The area to the east of the Salisbury Avon and south of the Kennet is still sparsely populated but numbers appear to be increasing.

It still appears to be uncommon in the extreme west. It forms moderately large flocks especially in hard winters, up to c. 300 having been recorded. Song may be heard in mild winters and some males are apparently resident in their territories throughout the year.

PART TWO — NON-BREEDING BIRDS

RED-THROATED DIVER *Gavia stellata*

Vagrant.

There were three records for the previous century. Since 1947 there have been fifteen including a single bird that wintered in the Ashton Keynes area from December 1971 until April 1972.

A diver at Shearwater in February 1953 was at first thought to have been a Great Northern but was most probably of this species. One spent three weeks at Coate Water and Liden Lagoon during March 1979.

BLACK-THROATED DIVER *Gavia arctica*

Rare vagrant.

One was shot at Salisbury in December 1872 and another, undated, was killed at about the same time on the lake at Corsham Court. In 1942 one was found dead in Ogbourne after flying into overhead wires during a snowstorm. A single bird spent several days on a gravel pit (AK 6/7) at Ashton Keynes in December 1972 and there was one at Coate Water in February 1978.

There were a number of records in 1979 the first being an immature at Winterslow on 17th February. Unfortunately this bird was subsequently found dead. From 18th February there was a series of records in the Water Park up to 18th March. At least two and probably three birds were involved in sightings on several gravel pits in the Ashton Keynes area.

GREAT NORTHERN DIVER *Gavia immer*

Vagrant.

Smith lists eleven records for the last century and there are five, all recent, for this century. Of these latter one was reported by the Keeper at Coate Water in March 1946 and another was found dead there in November 1952.

An adult was found sitting in a puddle at a road junction in West Kennet during November 1962. This bird was cared for at Marlborough College for a few days and then released at Wilton Water. One spent nearly a month on a gravel pit (AK 6) at Ashton Keynes during November and December 1970. An adult was present at Fonthill Lake in December 1977.

RED-NECKED GREBE *Podiceps grisegena*

Vagrant.

Apparently thirteen records. Only five records for this century: a party of three birds on the Avon near Britford in January 1934; and single birds at Coate Water during February and March 1955, December 1978 and March 1979; and one at Corsham Lake from mid-February to mid-March 1979.

SLAVONIAN GREBE *Podiceps auritus*

Vagrant

There are six records from the last century and so far this century there have been ten. The records have been widespread throughout the county. Longleat January 1958; Wroughton Reservoir November 1962; Salisbury March 1967 and February 1973; Coate Water December 1968; Wilton Water 1969; Erlestoke December 1969 and at Easton Royal in January 1971. During 1947 a bird was present on the Kennet near Overton from mid May to early September. A single bird present from February to April 1979 on a pit at Somerford Keynes occasionally visited the Wiltshire end of it.

Peirson, 1957, suggests that early records of this species may have been confused with those of the following species. This would appear unlikely as the majority of records concerned specimens.

BLACK-NECKED GREBE *Podiceps nigricollis*

Vagrant.

There are eighteen records, seven from the last century and eleven from this. The majority have been at Coate Water: September 1945, November 1969, January/February 1974, February 1976 and March 1979; and Corsham Lake May 1962, December 1969 and August 1979; Bowood Lake November 1964; Kent End April 1978; Liden Lagoon February 1979.

There are one or two poorly documented recent records that could refer to this or to the previous species.

FULMAR *Fulmarus glacialis*

Very rare vagrant.

An immature was found in the forest near Marlborough in October 1897. An adult at Boscombe Down on the 30th January 1978 died on the following day. Another at Coate Water in June of the same year.

MANX SHEARWATER *Puffinus puffinus*

Rare vagrant.

There are only eight records of this species, all comparatively recent. The first was found at Brinkworth in 1948. This bird had been ringed at Skokholm, Pembrokeshire, on 2nd September and was recovered five days later. The second record also involved a Skokholm bird, one that had been taken to Cambridge in July 1951 for release as part of a "homing" experiment. Unfortunately this bird was shot and killed near Westbury whilst presumably returning to its nesting burrow on Skokholm.

Other records were at Market Lavington 1962; Colerne and Lyneham airfields 1967; Highworth 1968; Lyneham 1975; and Salisbury 1977. All but one were recorded in September, those critically examined being birds of the year.

WILSON'S PETREL *Oceanites oceanicus*

Very rare vagrant.

A single record of a bird found freshly dead at Sutton Benger in November 1849. This specimen was almost lost when the original finder threw the bird away thinking it to be a Swift.

STORM PETREL *Hydrobates pelagicus*

Rare vagrant.

A total of eight records of which four are from this century. All records are of birds "picked up" after storms and include one at Marlborough in 1929 and one at Redlynch in April 1951.

LEACH'S PETREL *Oceanodroma leucorhoa*

Rare vagrant.

There were five reported in the last century most of these being found dead or dying. In late October and early November 1952 twelve birds were found in various parts of the county, victims of the "wreck" which distributed a larger number throughout the British Isles. There have been three subsequent records: one found dead at Keevil in December 1962, another in poor condition at Longleat in March 1965 and one still capable of flight near Calne in December 1979.

GANNET *Sula bassana*
Vagrant.

There are thirteen records. The six during this century have been at Potterne August 1952; Pewsham August and Rowde September 1953; Chippenham April 1958; Tan Hill June 1971; West Dean November 1976. One spent several days in the Water Park during April 1977 before being shot by an irate fisherman. A sub-adult was seen in flight near Shrewton in September 1978.

CORMORANT *Phalacrocorax carbo*
Regular visitor.

At least ten were recorded in the last century but this species can now be considered a regular visitor to the county. It is most often seen in the Salisbury area and in the Water Park but Bowood Lake, Braydon Pond, Coate Water and Shearwater are also visited but less frequently. These have mainly been single birds but double figures have been recorded at favoured sites. One ringed as a nestling at Bodorgan, Anglesey in May 1969 was recovered at Box in September 1969.

SHAG Phalacrocorax aristotelis
Vagrant.

A total of twelve records, three in the last century. Recent records have been mainly in the north of the county and include: Swindon area December 1957, April 1962, November 1963, October 1971 and November 1975; Marlborough October 1922, March 1962; Great Bedwyn November 1975; Shearwater January 1958.

BITTERN *Botaurus stellaris*

Winter visitor (uncommon).

At least one record in most winters, more often in the Salisbury Avon Valley. Booming was heard at Coate Water when the reed beds were more extensive during the early 1950s. Rather more records in the winter of 1978/79, at least seven individuals being recorded.

LITTLE BITTERN *Ixobrychus minutus*

Rare vagrant.

There were four records for last century: at Stourton 1820; Seend 1850; Britford 1851 and Wilton 1869. The only recent record is of a bird found dead on Salisbury Plain in March 1940.

NIGHT HERON *Nycticorax nycticorax*

Very rare vagrant.

Five records, but only two really satisfactory: an immature at Longford in October 1956 and an adult at Coate Water in April 1978. One reputedly seen at Lake on an unspecified date, a possible at Longford in May 1954. The Rawlence collection contained a specimen supposedly taken near Downton with no other details.

SQUACCO HERON *Ardeola ralloides*

Very rare vagrant.

Two, possibly three records. One at Boynton 1775 and another at Britford. A specimen in the Rawlence collection supposedly killed in Wiltshire but no locality quoted.

WHITE STORK *Ciconia ciconia*

Rare vagrant.

Some eight records of which one was in the eighteenth and two in the nineteenth century. One at Downton 1789; Codford 1882 and one undated, killed near Salisbury. All the records this century are comparatively recent: Downton June 1952; Upavon April 1967; East Knoyle June 1971 and two birds at Ashton Keynes in September 1972; the latest a single bird at Stockton in August 1975.

GLOSSY IBIS *Plegadis falcinellus*

Very rare vagrant.

Only two records. One was killed near Calne in 1825. Two were present at Burderop Park in September 1915; one of these was shot and preserved.

SPOONBILL *Platalea leucorodia*

Very rare vagrant.

There are only two records, both being in 1978. Two birds were present at Coate Water for a few hours in April and a single bird was seen in the Cotswold Water Park near Ashton Keynes in July.

BEWICK'S SWAN *Cygnus columbianus*

Winter visitor (uncommon).

This species had not been observed in the county until 1954 when a party of eight visited Fonthill Lake in February. A single bird remained for several days after the others had moved on. The second record was a single bird at Coate Water in February 1955.

The cold winter of early 1956 produced an influx of nearly 40 birds on six waters during the period February/April. In December of the same year 11 birds were reported from Coate Water and Braydon Pond.

With the exception of 1958, 1962 and 1969 there have been records in every year since, up to and including 1979. In 1977 a bird fell dead on to a school playing field in Swindon.

WHOOPER SWAN *Cygnus cygnus*
Vagrant.

There are nineteen records of this species. Five of these were for the last century, the remaining fourteen for this. All of the latter have been since 1947. Only recorded after very cold or stormy conditions and widely spread throughout the county.

BEAN GOOSE *Anser fabalis*
Very rare vagrant.

There is a single record of this species at Amesbury in December 1966. From its behaviour it may well have been an escaped bird.

PINK-FOOTED GOOSE *Anser brachyrhynchus*
Rare vagrant.

There are six records for this century: one shot at Imber in February 1952; Chitterne January/April 1961; Maiden Bradley January 1964; a small flock of c. 14 at Little Bedwyn January 1964 and a single bird at Corsham Lake in October 1970.

WHITE-FRONTED GOOSE *Anser albifrons*
Winter visitor (irregular).

Recorded in most winters in small numbers. Surprisingly, Smith had no definite records of this species for the nineteenth century. Grey geese are not uncommonly seen in flight during the winter and the majority are probably of this species.

LESSER WHITE-FRONTED GOOSE *Anser erythropus*
Very rare vagrant.

There are two records of this species: an adult on the River Wylye near Bathampton House in March 1976; the other was at Coate Water in April 1977. As this species is widely kept in captivity both records probably involved escaped birds.

SNOW GOOSE *Anser caerulescens*

Vagrant (escape).

There have been three records all presumably relating to "escaped" birds. One at Wilton Water April 1970; one at Kent End August 1973 and a flock of six at Coate Water during the spring of 1977.

BARNACLE GOOSE *Branta leucopsis*

Rare vagrant.

Two records prior to 1900. Two were killed at Enford in February 1865 and another undated at Britford. There have been five records this century: one at Bowood Lake January 1957; Longford April 1959; Wilton Water November 1969 and regularly there until late 1971. One found dead South Marston April 1974; Lacock February 1975. Since 1976 there have been a number of records in the Water Park concerning this species and several hybrids have been seen.

It is quite possible that all records, particularly the more recent, refer to escapes from captivity.

BRENT GOOSE *Branta bernicla*

Rare vagrant.

There were five records for the last century all represented by specimens: one on the Salisbury Avon February 1870; West Lavington October 1881; Collingbourne winter 1881/82; Britford 1884 and Collingbourne 1887. Only one record this century, at Clarendon Lake December 1933.

RUDDY SHELDUCK *Tadorna ferruginea*

Very rare vagrant.

Only five records and all may have been escapes from captivity. One on the Salisbury Avon at Longford in April 1928; one Clarendon Lake April 1946 and one at Coate Water in

November 1968. A flock of four was seen in the Water Park at various locations in September 1979 and a single female in the same area in February 1980.

SHELDUCK *Tadorna tadorna*

Irregular visitor.

Occurs infrequently mainly on larger waters and gravel pits. More usual in winter but also spring and autumn.

One present at Coate Water from early autumn 1976 paired with a female Mallard in the springs of 1977 and 1978.

A bird ringed on the Grosser Knechtsand in West Germany in August 1969 was recovered near Cricklade in October 1972.

WIGEON *Anas penelope*

Winter visitor.

A regular winter visitor usually in small numbers on the majority of larger waters and marshes.

Occasionally larger flocks are seen particularly in the Water Park in January and February.

AMERICAN WIGEON *Anas americana*

Very rare vagrant.

A single record of two males at the confluence of the Rivers Avon and Frome in August 1976. In view of the date both were presumably escapes from captivity.

GADWALL *Anas strepera*

Winter visitor.

A very rare visitor in the last century with only two records. Up to 1957 there were a further eight records. Since then numbers have increased with, until recently, quite a large wintering flock at Fonthill Lake and a smaller one in the Water Park. Individuals and small parties have been more regular on most of the larger lakes.

The last two or three years have seen a decline particularly in the Fonthill wintering flock.

PINTAIL *Anas acuta*

Winter visitor (uncommon).

Seen in very small parties or singly in most winters, more often only males being identified. Has occurred on all the larger waters.

GARGANEY *Anas querquedula*

Passage migrant.

Has apparently decreased this century and is now an uncommon migrant seen mainly in March and April. There is no evidence to suggest that it has ever bred in the county.

RING-NECKED DUCK *Aythya collaris*

Very rare vagrant.

A male was present at Corsham Lake for several days in January and on one date in February 1978; what may have been the same male was at Ashton Keynes in April of the same year.

FERRUGINOUS DUCK *Aythya nyroca*

Very rare vagrant.

There are only three records: two birds at Netheravon in December 1875 and one undated at Lake House (Smith). One was present on the Kennet at Mildenhall in February 1971.

SCAUP *Aythya marila*

Vagrant.

There are only sixteen records of this duck but several of these refer to more than one individual. Of the more recent records three were at Coate Water, April 1957, April 1961 and March 1962; Chilton Foliat January 1959 and January 1964; Corsham Lake March 1975; Stourton January 1958; Ashton Keynes December 1970; Westbury 1970; a female at Coate Water in November and a male there in December 1978 into January 1979.

EIDER *Somateria mollissima*

Very rare vagrant.

Only two records, both from the last century. One (undated) was shot at Lyneham and the other near Woodborough in March 1866.

LONG-TAILED DUCK *Clangula hyemalis*

Rare vagrant.

Five records, all in this century. Single birds recorded at Petersfinger October 1950; Grafton November 1962; Corsham Lake December 1967, January 1974; Ashton Keynes March/May 1974.

COMMON SCOTER *Melanitta nigra*
Vagrant.

Apparently four records for the last century and fifteen for this. Of recent records, six were in March and April, three in October, two in January, with singles in February, July, August and November.

VELVET SCOTER *Melanitta fusca*
Very rare vagrant.

Four records, one shot at Mildenhall October 1885; Marlborough October 1889; a male at Ashton Keynes December 1959; an adult male at Coate Water and Liden Lagoon January 1979.

GOLDENEYE *Bucephala clangula*
Winter visitor.

Until recently it was an uncommon winter visitor and passage migrant. During the past ten years it has increased, particularly in the north. In recent years the Water Park wintering population has exceeded forty birds, normally less than half of these in Wiltshire.

SMEW *Mergus albellus*
Vagrant.

A single record for the last century, one killed at Fyfield in January 1876. There seem to be sixteen records this century. At Ashton Keynes, 'red-heads' February/March 1976, December 1977 and January 1979; at Coate Water singles in 1939, 1945 and a female November 1977. There were two, possibly three, males at Coate in December 1952. There were singles at Corsham Lake in November 1962 and March 1976; a single 'red-head' at Tockenham February 1976; a male and two 'red-heads' on the Avon near Dauntsey in January 1963; Longleat, a single in March 1958 and January 1962, a male and two 'red-heads' there in March 1963 (probably the same birds seen at Dauntsey the same year). A single 'red-head' Liden Lagoon February/March 1978 and another there in February 1979.

RED-BREASTED MERGANSER *Mergus serrator*
Vagrant.

There were five records for the nineteenth century and there are several for this. The more recent records are: three on the Salisbury Avon February 1947; one at Longford and nearby gravel pits February 1956; Fonthill January 1958; c. 70 in flight Idmiston March 1961; Tockenham November 1963; Wilton Water December 1975. A single at Coate February 1976 and a female on the Station Pond at Westbury February 1979.

GOOSANDER *Mergus merganser*
Winter visitor (uncommon).

Occurs most winters, singly or in small parties generally on the larger waters and occasionally on the Salisbury and Bristol Avons. It has been slightly more numerous in recent years and 1979 saw numbers of up to 19 at Coate Water and eight at Ashton Keynes.

HONEY BUZZARD *Pernis apivorus*
Vagrant.

Some eight records for the last century, several undated, but all were shot and preserved. There are only three records for this century. One was shot near Wilsford during the last war and another was seen in flight near Tilshead in May 1963. Two were seen in flight over Swindon in September 1978.

WHITE-TAILED EAGLE *Haliaeetus albicilla*

Very rare vagrant.

Only two records for this century: at Grovely Wood in March 1905 and Morden in February 1909.

During the last century one was shot at Littlecote whilst feeding on a dead doe in January 1847. Another was killed in Braydon Forest December 1841; one near Marlborough in 1859. (In 1828 or '29 a bird supposedly of this species roosted overnight on the spire of Salisbury Cathedral.)

MARSH HARRIER *Circus aeruginosus*

Rare vagrant.

Smith states that it was formerly "not uncommon" but he could only list the following records. One undated at Salisbury; two undated Kingston Deverill; one Easton October 1876; Netheravon August 1878. Six have been recorded since that last date, one at Braydon Pond March 1960, on Wylye Down November 1963, an immature Roundway Hill September 1977, females at Pewsey and Boyton in May 1978 and an immature near Bratton August/September 1979.

HEN HARRIER *Circus cyaneus*

Winter visitor.

Regular winter visitor to more open and upland areas of the county from October to May. In recent years the total winter population has been at least twelve and probably nearer twenty individuals. It is commoner now than in the nineteenth century and the first decades of this. Roosts have been located from time to time and up to seven birds have been observed at one of these.

GOSHAWK *Accipiter gentilis*

Vagrant

The status of this species is obscured by the fact that it is a popular falconers' bird and has been regularly flown in the county. Over the years some of these have been lost and may well account for most of the sight records.

One shot at Compton Bassett in September 1885 may well have been a wild bird. The more recent records were: Durnford October 1958; Chippenham April 1968; Swindon April and November 1969; Steeple Langford January/February 1970; Everleigh February 1971; Imber September 1974; Porton Down in February and September 1977.

ROUGH-LEGGED BUZZARD *Buteo lagopus*

Winter visitor (irregular).

There were at least twelve records for the latter half of the last century, most of these being of birds shot or trapped. (A pair reputedly bred near Tisbury in 1882, adults and young being killed and preserved, according to Smith.)

This century produced no satisfactory records until 1966 when a single bird was seen at Tilshead in October and another at Weavern in November and December. One was present at Weavern on two occasions in March 1967. All these records could apply to the same bird. There were records of single birds in 1968 at Edington in October, and at Rushall in January 1972.

There were three records in 1974 all of single birds: at Warren Down in April; Porton Down in October and at Wexcombe Down in December.

A major influx occurred in 1975. Up to three at Imber in February and March with a single bird being seen there in July and August. Five were present in the Ham, Buttermere area during March and April. Single birds were at Everleigh and Fyfield Down, and two at Porton – all in March. There was a single autumn record at Colerne airfield in September, possibly the Imber bird moving on. In 1977 there were single birds at Hippenscombe in October and at Woodfalls in November.

OSPREY *Pandion haliaetus*

Passage migrant.

Nine records for the last century, some of which concerned more than one individual; unfortunately the majority were killed. There were no records between 1883 and 1951, when one spent the summer at Fonthill Lake. Other records were at Great Durnford October 1956; on the Wylye mid-May 1967; Braydon Pond September 1967; Wylye, two present in June 1968; Wilton Water April and Calne September 1971; Erlestoke August, Ashton Keynes and Eysey September 1973; Shrewton September 1975; Chippenham April, two at Ashton Keynes October 1976; singles at Salisbury/Grovely Wood and Coate Water in late May 1977. One spent several days at Shearwater in July 1979 and an immature was seen at Rood Ashton Lake in August 1979. A migrating adult was seen in flight at Blunsdon in April 1980.

RED-FOOTED FALCON *Falco vespertinus*

Very rare vagrant.

There was a single doubtful record (undated) for the last century concerning a pair shot at Kingston Deverill. The first acceptable record was of a female near Orcheston Down in June 1973. There were a number of records in Southern England at this time.

GYRFALCON *Falco rusticolus*

Very rare vagrant.

Only two records. One was seen on the Ramscliffe near Market Lavington in December 1842. It was at first thought to be an albino Peregrine but was later ascribed to the race *F. r. islandus*. One shot at Downton in April 1906 was considered to be an immature of the race *F. r. candicans.*

RED GROUSE *Lagopus lagopus*

Rare vagrant (last century).

None since 1866 and only four records for the whole of the nineteenth century: Roundway Park and Compton Bassett, undated; East Knoyle 1848 and Wedhampton 1866.

WATER RAIL *Rallus aquaticus*

Winter visitor.

Regular and locally common during winter with a very few records between May and August. It has not yet been proved to breed in the county although an immature was found dead near Melksham in August 1951.

CRANE *Grus grus*

Very rare vagrant.

Only two records, both recent. The first was a single bird near Trowbridge in June 1969 and the second at All Cannings in April 1975.

LITTLE BUSTARD *Tetrax tetrax*

Very rare vagrant.

There are three records of this species. Two were seen near Netheravon in August 1877; one at Little Wishford from mid July until mid September 1946. One was shot on the Plain in May 1952.

OYSTERCATCHER *Haematopus ostralegus*

Passage migrant.

Only two were recorded in the last century and there was none in this until 1951. Since then there have been over twenty records, the majority being in spring and autumn.

CREAM-COLOURED COURSER *Cursorius cursor*

Very rare vagrant.

One shot on open downland near Tilshead in October 1855 and another at Erlestoke in October 1896.

COLLARED PRATINCOLE *Glareola pratincola*

Very rare vagrant.

Only two records: one shot near Tilshead in October 1852 and a sight record of one hawking insects over the Thames at Cricklade in May 1968.

RINGED PLOVER *Charadrius hiaticula*

Passage migrant.

Until recently this species was an uncommon visitor but it has become a regular passage migrant particularly in the north of the county and Water Park.

KENTISH PLOVER *Charadrius alexandrinus*

Very rare vagrant.

There have been two recent records in the Water Park at pits adjacent to the county boundary but both in Gloucestershire. Both of these birds overflew into Wiltshire which would apparently qualify them for inclusion in this list. One was near Cerney Wick in May 1975 and the other between Ashton Keynes and

Somerford Keynes in May 1977. One in the Water Park, near South Cerney in May 1980, was apparently based in Wiltshire throughout its stay.

DOTTEREL *Charadrius morinellus*

Passage migrant.

Formerly a common spring and autumn migrant, both Smith and Marsh commenting on its abundance. By 1887 it had become uncommon and during this century it has steadily decreased. There have been only four recent sight records: a single at Bishopstone (Swindon) April and May 1951; near Chippenham in April 1955; a trip of five near Pitton in early May 1976 and a single at Fosbury in May 1977.

GOLDEN PLOVER *Pluvialis apricaria*

Winter visitor.

A locally common winter visitor particularly in traditionally favoured areas. The largest flocks occur in the north of the county, up to 2,000 frequenting the north-western slopes of the Marlborough Downs. Another large flock can be found in the Thames Valley usually between Cricklade and Ashton Keynes.

Other smaller flocks are found near Keevil, Old Sarum, Wilsford and other downland areas particularly between heights of 250 and 500 feet.

GREY PLOVER *Pluvialis squatarola*

Rare vagrant.

There are only six records of this species, all recent. Two were present at Coate Water in November 1934; singles at High Post April 1958; Hodson December 1962; Biddestone March 1963; Kent End June 1975 and two at Ashton Keynes (AK 6) May 1977.

KNOT *Calidris canutus*

Rare vagrant.

There are only seven records. Smith quotes three, Langley 1850; Seend February 1870 and at Langford in December 1879. One was caught in Salisbury during February 1906. Recent records include one at Coate Water in November 1956; another there in September 1960 and another single at Coombe Bissett in February 1963.

SANDERLING *Calidris alba*

Rare vagrant.

There are only six records. A small party on the By Brook at Ford in April 1960; eleven at Kent End in May 1973; two at the same site May 1976; three at the Liden Lagoon, Swindon in June 1977; one at Coate Water in August 1977 and up to two near South Cerney in May 1980.

LITTLE STINT *Calidris minuta*

Vagrant.

First recorded in September 1956 when two were present at Coate Water. There have been at least a further fifteen records since. At Coate Water in September 1960 and September 1975; Swindon sewage farm, September 1963, September 1969, two separate records there September 1974, September 1975 and three there 1978. Up to eight were present at Kent End in September and October 1976, also a single in August of the same year. This site also provided the only spring record, three being present there in June 1976. Four were present at Swindon sewage farm in September 1978.

TEMMINCK'S STINT *Calidris temminckii*

Very rare vagrant.

Only three records, two of these at Swindon sewage farm: one in August and September 1970, this bird being trapped and examined in the hand; the other in September 1974. The third record was of a single bird at Calne Sand Pits in September 1978.

PECTORAL SANDPIPER *Calidris melanotos*

Very rare vagrant.

There are only two records of this North American wader: a single bird was present on various gravel pits in the Ashton Keynes/Somerford Keynes areas during October 1976 and another was seen at Ashton Keynes in early October 1977.

CURLEW SANDPIPER *Calidris ferruginea*

Rare vagrant.

Smith lists one at Chippenham in July 1869. There were no more until 1958 when one was present at Coate Water in September. Other records include one at Coate Water August 1959, another there September 1960, up to three at Swindon sewage farm in August and September 1969, and a single there in September 1974.

PURPLE SANDPIPER *Calidris maritima*

Very rare vagrant.

Smith records one at Everleigh February 1881.

DUNLIN *Calidris alpina*

Irregular visitor.

There were few records for the last century and the early years of this. Since the 1940s it has become a more frequent visitor. The majority have occurred in autumn but it is not uncommon in winter at favoured sites. It is rather less common in spring, generally only single birds. Regularly visited sites include Coate Water, Swindon sewage farm and the Water Park.

BROAD-BILLED SANDPIPER *Limicola falcinellus*

Very rare vagrant.

Only two records, both at Swindon sewage farm. The first was in September 1962 and the second in September 1977.

BUFF-BREASTED SANDPIPER *Tryngites subruficollis*
Very rare vagrant.

A single bird at Kent End in September 1975, a year in which many individuals of this American species were seen in this country.

RUFF *Philomachus pugnax*
Passage migrant.

From being a very rare vagrant, with only five records up to 1957, it now occurs most years, generally in ones and twos. An exception was the flock of twenty at Swindon sewage farm in September 1974. Winter visitors have occurred along the county boundary in the Water Park and on open downland with Lapwings.

JACK SNIPE *Lymnocryptes minimus*
Winter visitor.

An uncommon winter visitor usually in ones and twos. It occasionally occurs in larger numbers at such sites as Swindon sewage farm. Regular at Coate Water, Corsham Lake, Lacock and Swindon sewage farm. There are one or two records from downland areas.

GREAT SNIPE *Gallinago media*
Rare vagrant.

Smith records the following birds, all shot: one at Winterslow 1831; near Salisbury 1854; Hurdcott and Pewsey 1868; Hungerdown 1874. Two were shot this century, both at Britford, in 1933 and 1936. There have been several sight records since that may have referred to this species.

LONG-BILLED DOWITCHER *Limnodromus scolopaceus*

Very rare vagrant.

A single individual was present at Swindon sewage farm for some eleven days in September 1974.

BLACK-TAILED GODWIT *Limosa limosa*

Vagrant.

First recorded at Coate Water in August 1944 with further records since at: Whittonditch, Ramsbury April 1951; Cricklade January 1959; Hornham April 1959; Durrington December 1965; Chitterne Marsh and Axford June 1967; River Bourne March 1969; Coate Water 1971; on the county boundary at Shorncotes August 1975; Kent End August 1976; Coate Water March and September 1977; Britford October 1977; at Odstock March, Ashton Keynes April and Coate Water early and late August, 1978; in 1979 a party of twelve visited Kent End, Ashton Keynes briefly in April and a single bird was present at Coate in May.

The flock at Durrington comprised some 250 birds and was featured on Southern Television.

BAR-TAILED GODWIT *Limosa lapponica*

Vagrant.

Smith could list only one record, near Marlborough in November 1881.

There have been six records so far this century. At Coate Water in July 1958, September 1975, March and October 1976; Leckford April 1969; and Avebury March 1970.

WHIMBREL *Numenius phaeopus*

Passage migrant (uncommon).

Up to 1957 Peirson could list only five records for this century. Since that date there have been well over twenty and it is now an annual migrant in very small numbers.

This change in the frequency of reports may be due to an increase in observers rather than an increase in birds.

SPOTTED REDSHANK *Tringa erythropus*
Passage migrant.

First recorded in February 1947 at Charlton Mill and since then there have been over 25 records, the majority in August or September. In addition to the February record above there are two for March, at Kent End, Ashton Keynes in 1975 and at Coate Water in 1976.

With only two exceptions all the records have been in the north of the county.

GREENSHANK *Tringa nebularia*
Passage migrant.

Regular passage migrant in small numbers, most frequent in May, August and September. Coate Water, Corsham Lake, Fonthill, Swindon sewage farm and the Water Park are popular sites.

SOLITARY SANDPIPER *Tringa solitaria*

Very rare vagrant.

There is a single record of this transatlantic vagrant. One was present at Swindon sewage farm for several days in early September 1966. The bird was trapped and ringed during its stay.

GREEN SANDPIPER *Tringa ochropus*

Passage migrant and winter visitor.

A common autumn passage migrant in the north of the county, particularly at Swindon sewage farm and the Water Park. Much less common elsewhere, being quite rare in some apparently suitable southern areas. Winters regularly but in ones and twos only, usually in the north.

The spring passage is much less obvious than that in July and August but tends to be more widespread.

WOOD SANDPIPER *Tringa glareola*

Passage migrant (uncommon).

Only one record for the last century, at Lavington in January 1879. There were no satisfactory records this century until August 1952. Since then there have been over thirty records, several of these involving more than one individual. The majority have been in August and September but there is a single April record, four in May and two in June. Only two of these are from areas south of the Marlborough Downs.

TURNSTONE *Arenaria interpres*

Very rare vagrant.

Although occurring on passage in neighbouring counties this species managed to avoid detection in Wiltshire until 1973. A single bird was then seen at Kent End in May of that year and other singles there in June and July 1975. During 1976 there were singles at Ashton Keynes in April, Kent End in May and two at Coate Water in September. There were up to three near South Cerney in May 1980.

RED-NECKED PHALAROPE *Phalaropus lobatus*
Very rare vagrant.

Only one record, a male shot near Devizes in May 1841.

GREY PHALAROPE *Phalaropus fulicarius*
Vagrant.

There were at least twenty records for the last century and a very few for the earlier years of this. The only recent records include single birds near Lyneham in October 1954; Coate Water October 1960; Winterbourne Dauntsey November 1963, and near Devizes in January 1974.

POMARINE SKUA *Stercorarius pomarinus*
Very rare vagrant.

An immature was shot at Sherston about 1885, the specimen being preserved.

ARCTIC SKUA *Stercorarius parasiticus*
Rare vagrant.

One shot near Pewsey in November 1867; one at Heytesbury in October 1879 and another near Mortinsell in 1881. Records for this century include one found dead beneath high tension cables at Wilsford in October 1938; an immature on the Wiltshire/Gloucestershire border near South Cerney January 1974. Three in flight, most probably of this species, over Little Durnsford in early September 1976. An immature, probably of this species, at Boscombe Down in October 1978.

LONG-TAILED SKUA *Stercorarius longicaudus*

Very rare vagrant.

One was found dead at Calstone in May 1881.

GREAT SKUA *Stercorarius skua*

Very rare vagrant.

Ten records up to 1885 but there has been none since.

MEDITERRANEAN GULL *Larus melanocephalus*

Very rare vagrant.

Only one record, a single bird at Hilperton in February 1973.

LITTLE GULL *Larus minutus*

Vagrant.

There were three records in the last century: one at Rodbourne, Swindon 1848; one at Upton Scudamore January 1869 and one at Rockley in March 1870. One at Knowle in 1935; one found dead near Savernake Station February 1950. At Coate Water December 1964 to March 1965; at Coate Water again in September 1973 and April 1975; Ashton Keynes in February 1975; Coate Water March and September 1976; Kent End in May 1976. Also at Coate January and October 1977, May 1978 and May 1979; and an immature at Liden Lagoon, Swindon January 1979.

BLACK-HEADED GULL *Larus ridibundus*

Regular visitor.

A widespread and common visitor and, rather like the Common Gull, tends to divide into three separate groups: those to the south of the Vale of Pewsey roosting on the Solent, those in the west roosting at Chew Valley Lake, and the northern birds in the Water Park at South Cerney.

Immatures are present during the summer but usually only in small numbers.

There has been a large increase in the wintering population during the past 25 years.

COMMON GULL *Larus canus*

Regular visitor.

A very common winter visitor seemingly divided into two distinct groups by the Pewsey Vale. Those to the north roost on the Severn and those to the south on the Solent. The birds use regular flight lines to their roosts, these being very obvious in the north during winter. A very few can be seen in summer, these usually being first-summer birds. It has greatly increased in the county during the past twenty years.

LESSER BLACK-BACKED GULL *Larus fuscus*

Regular visitor.

Seen frequently on spring and autumn passage and quite large flocks summer at a few sites. Up to 500 can be found at Swindon rubbish tip and smaller flocks occur in the Trowbridge, Keevil and Kingston Deverill areas. Numbers are much lower in winter but occurrences are more widespread. Individuals of the race *L. f. graellsii* have been identified during both spring and autumn passage.

HERRING GULL *Larus argentatus*

Regular visitor.

Much less common than the previous species but commoner now than in the past. It is more frequent in autumn and winter with small parties in the Chippenham, Trowbridge, Salisbury and Swindon areas. The large gull roost in the Water Park seldom includes more than 40 individuals of this species.

ICELAND GULL *Larus glaucoides*

Very rare vagrant.

One at Erlestoke in January 1973. Another "white" gull seen at Wilton Water at about the same time was not specifically identified but may well have been the same individual.

GREAT BLACK-BACKED GULL *Larus marinus*

Irregular visitor.

Infrequent during the last century, uncommon in this until 1930. Since then it has been recorded in most years, generally singly and more often in autumn.

KITTIWAKE *Rissa tridactyla*

Vagrant.

There were a few records in the last century, and seven since March 1953 when one was found dead at Longleat. Others were found at the same site in April 1955 and May 1957. Remains were found at Tockenham in May 1957. Also recorded at Longford in January 1958; Charlton February 1959 and Salisbury in January 1965.

IVORY GULL *Pagophila eburnea*

Very rare vagrant.

One shot near Chippenham about 1840. This record was listed in Hony's Notes on the Birds of Wiltshire (BB VII, 281-290) but there is little supporting evidence.

SANDWICH TERN *Sterna sandvicensis*

Vagrant.

The first record was of two at Erlestoke Lake in April 1947. There have been seven more records since: at Coate Water in

April 1949; Swindon August 1958; Tockenham Reservoir June 1964; Wilton Water October 1971; Steeple Langford May 1972 and Kent End August 1975. There were two at Liden Lagoon in September 1978.

ROSEATE TERN *Sterna dougallii*

Very rare vagrant.

Only one record. A dazed but apparently uninjured bird found on a garden path at Seagry August 1964. It had been ringed in County Wexford, Eire on the 30th June 1962.

ARCTIC TERN *Sterna paradisaea*

Passage migrant (regular).

Reported regularly in very small numbers in spring and autumn mainly from Coate Water, Corsham Lake and in the Water Park. An immature that had been ringed in Estonia on the 20th June 1956 was recovered at Little Somerford on the 4th September 1956 after breaking a wing against a fisherman's rod.

LITTLE TERN *Sterna albifrons*

Vagrant.

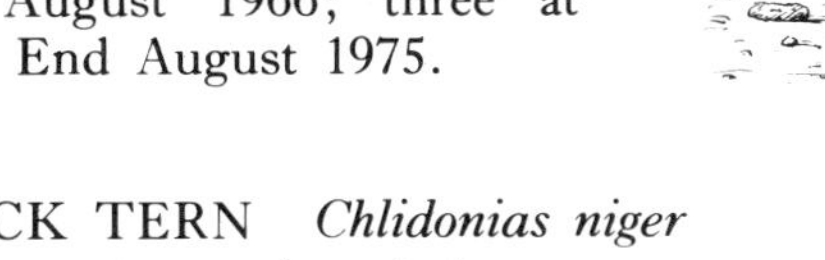

Seven records, the first at Rood Ashton in April 1912. One at Britford March 1928; Stratford April 1934; at Coate Water August 1956, May 1958 and August 1966; three at Kent End August 1975.

BLACK TERN *Chlidonias niger*

Passage migrant (regular).

Now seen regularly on both spring and autumn passage; formerly more usual in spring and in smaller numbers. Coate Water, Corsham Lake and the Water Park are regularly visited. It is usually in ones and twos but occasionally into double figures.

GUILLEMOT *Uria aalge*

Rare vagrant.

Only three records: one shot at Salisbury in December 1871; one at Amesbury 1888 and one caught at Warminster in May 1916.

RAZORBILL *Alca torda*

Rare vagrant.

Five records all from last century. One at Melksham February 1862; Netheravon January 1866; Chitterne January 1871; Salisbury end of 1871 and Britford in February 1883.

LITTLE AUK *Alle alle*

Rare vagrant.

Four records from the last century. One at Ogbourne and Clatford 1864; one at Gore Cross in October 1869; Wilsford Down October 1870. Records for this century include singles at Grovely Wood and Winterbourne December 1912.

Eight individuals were found at scattered localities in February and March 1950, victims of a major "wreck". The only recent record is of one at High Post in November 1961.

PUFFIN *Fratercula arctica*

Vagrant.

At least seven records for the last century and nine for this. The majority occurred in late autumn and winter but there were two August records.

PALLAS'S SANDGROUSE *Syrrhaptes paradoxus*

Very rare vagrant.

One killed at Imber in June 1863 and a party of about twenty were present in May 1888. Both these years saw large invasions of this species into western Europe.

SCOPS OWL *Otus scops*

Very rare vagrant.

Smith lists three records: one killed in the south of the county about 1835; one undated at Kingston Deverill and another at Wilton in the spring of 1873.

SNOWY OWL *Nyctea scandiaca*

Very rare vagrant.

One sight record, near Marlborough in January 1945.

HAWK OWL *Surnia ulula*

Very rare vagrant.

Only one, a bird shot at Amesbury about 1850.

ALPINE SWIFT *Apus melba*

Very rare vagrant.

One in flight over the River Wylye and water meadows near Stapleford October 1927. One was seen with Swifts in Gloucestershire but on the county boundary at Shorncotes sewage farm in June 1977.

BEE-EATER *Merops apiaster*

Very rare vagrant.

One shot at Bishopstrow near Warminster in May 1866.

ROLLER *Coracias garrulus*

Very rare vagrant.

One seen in Savernake Forest in 1883 and another on the Wiltshire/Hampshire border near Bramshaw in late September and early October 1947.

ROCK PIPIT *Anthus spinoletta*

Passage migrant.

The race *A. s. spinoletta* was first identified in the county at Swindon sewage farm in March 1955. Since that time there have been records at Bincknoll March 1967; High Deverill March 1972; Coate Water April 1973, March/April 1976; Swindon sewage farm March 1976; Ashton Keynes (AK 7) April 1976;

Longbridge Deverill January/March 1977 and Britford December 1977; three at Britford January and singles there in February and March 1978; one at Fovant watercress beds January/February and three there in March 1978; two in the Water Park, Kent End, April 1978.

There have been three records of *A. s. petrosus*: at Coate Water in March 1976, at Ashton Keynes (AK 6) in October 1977 and one at Liden Lagoon, Swindon in October 1979.

WAXWING *Bombycilla garrulus*

Winter visitor.

An occasional winter visitor. When it does occur the flocks are very small, often only one or two birds. Since Peirson's list in 1957 there have been the following records: Porton Down two in February 1959; East Knoyle a single December 1961/January 1962; a single at Longford January 1963; several records November/December 1966 at Chippenham, Collingbourne Ducis, Ford, Lackham, Marlborough, Salisbury and Shalbourne; also at Hindon in December 1966; Lyneham January and Savernake April 1966.

BLUETHROAT *Luscinia svecica*

Very rare vagrant.

The first county record was of a female in a garden at Idmiston in late May 1959. The second concerned another female at Swindon sewage farm in late August 1972. This bird was trapped and ringed. Early in September of the same year a male of the race *L. s. cyanecula* was seen at the same site. This bird was still present on 7th October.

RING OUZEL *Turdus torquatus*

Passage migrant.

In recent years it has been seen on spring passage more frequently than in autumn. Numbers are always small, usually single birds seen on higher ground particularly on the Marlborough Downs.

There is one doubtful breeding record in 1868.

FIELDFARE *Turdus pilaris*

Winter visitor.

Normally arrives in October departing in late April with stragglers into May.

Whilst the weather remains mild the high ground is occupied by large flocks. Cold weather soon moves these flocks down into more enclosed areas where hawthorn berries are more available. If hard weather continues for more than a few days numbers dwindle rapidly as the birds move on.

Large winter roosts have been located at Erlestoke, Grovely Wood, Somerford Common and Water Eaton Copse.

A bird ringed in Sweden in May 1952 was recovered at Chilmark in December 1952. Extreme arrival and departure dates are 7th August 1958 and 28th May 1970.

REDWING *Turdus iliacus*

Winter visitor.

Like the Fieldfare this species normally arrives in October but there are a few September records. Departure is usually in late March or early April.

Quite large flocks form in autumn but these tend to disperse into smaller groups as the winter progresses.

It is very susceptible to hard weather and many die in hard winters. Mortality was very high during the winters of 1916/17, 1929, 1947 and 1962/63.

It often shares roosts with Fieldfares and other thrushes.

Birds ringed in the county have been recovered in Russia, Finland, Italy and France.

Extreme arrival and departure dates are 20th September 1963 and 21st May 1978.

SAVI'S WARBLER *Locustella luscinioides*

Very rare vagrant.

A single bird was present at Coate Water from early May 1965 until at least the end of the month. It was trapped and ringed during its stay.

AQUATIC WARBLER *Acrocephalus paludicola*

Very rare vagrant.

The first county record was of a bird trapped at Coate Water in September 1958. The second and third records were at Swindon sewage farm in September 1970 and September/October 1972.

ICTERINE WARBLER *Hippolais icterina*

Very rare vagrant.

One was seen and heard singing at Salisbury in July 1944. (The species reputedly bred at Mildenhall in May 1970.)

MELODIOUS WARBLER *Hippolais polyglotta*

Very rare vagrant.

A single bird seen at Swindon sewage farm in September 1966.

YELLOW-BROWED WARBLER *Phylloscopus inornatus*

Very rare vagrant.

Only one record: a bird present in a garden at Trowbridge for a single day in October 1972.

FIRECREST *Regulus ignicapillus*

Vagrant.

There was a single record for the last century, in October 1881. The next record was not until March 1943, near Bulford. Since then there have been some twenty-five records between October and April. There are single records for May and September.

RED-BREASTED FLYCATCHER *Ficedula parva*

Very rare vagrant.

There is a single record of one near Calne in May 1944.

PIED FLYCATCHER *Ficedula hypoleuca*

Passage migrant.

A rare visitor in the last century and in the early years of this. It is now regularly reported in both spring and autumn.

Pairs have been seen in apparently suitable breeding habitat but a nest has not yet been found.

BEARDED TIT *Panurus biarmicus*

Rare vagrant.

First recorded at Corsham Lake, a female in October 1965 and subsequently two calling October 1970, one calling end of November and a female there December 1971; a female September 1972, two calling in January and a pair in March 1975, two males and a female mid October 1978. A pair at Swindon sewage farm October, two males and four females there mid October, finally a pair in November 1978. A male trapped at Lacock gravel pits late October 1973, a pair there October 1976. A bird ringed at Corsham in October 1978 was recovered at Pett Level, Sussex in November 1978.

GOLDEN ORIOLE *Oriolus oriolus*

Irregular visitor.

An uncommon visitor most often seen in spring, but there are a few summer and autumn records. There is some slight evidence to suggest that it may have bred in recent years.

LESSER GREY SHRIKE *Lanius minor*

Very rare vagrant.

One was present at Castle Eaton for two days in late June 1965, the only county record.

GREAT GREY SHRIKE *Lanius excubitor*

Winter visitor (uncommon).

It occurs most winters in favoured sites, particularly on the Plain, the Marlborough Downs and in the New Forest areas of the county. Those seen in enclosed lowland areas are probably on passage to rougher, more open country.

WOODCHAT SHRIKE *Lanius senator*

Rare vagrant.

Five records: at Salisbury 1872; Savernake Forest in June 1884; Aldbourne in June 1906; Fyfield Down September 1969 and an adult at Great Bradford Wood in July 1974.

NUTCRACKER *Nucifraga caryocatactes*

Rare vagrant.

Only three records and two of these probably refer to the same bird. One at the roadside near Warminster in September and a single bird seen on two occasions at Tollard Royal in October 1968 and January 1969. There was an unprecedented invasion of the slender-billed race *N. c. macrorhynchos* during the autumn of 1968.

CHOUGH *Pyrrhocorax pyrrhocorax*

Former vagrant.

Only five records, all early in the last century and each confirmed by a specimen. Localities were: Yatesbury, Battersby Camp, Lake, Tidworth and on the Plain.

ROSE-COLOURED STARLING *Sturnus roseus*
Rare vagrant.

There are only seven records: at Wilton 1853; near Bremhill 1868; near Box; Road Hill.

This century at Kingston Deverill March and Brinkworth July 1963; Bishopstone July 1972.

BRAMBLING *Fringilla montifringilla*
Winter visitor (irregular).

Most irregular in numbers, sometimes extremely numerous and in other winters very few are seen. Often seen in beech woods but feeds on stubble and in weed-grown rough ground. Seldom arrives before October, normally departing in March with stragglers into May. Earliest arrival date 30th September 1959 and latest departure 21st April 1968.

SISKIN *Carduelis spinus*
Winter visitor.

Formerly an uncommon and irregular visitor from early autumn until March or April. During the past fifteen years there has been a marked increase in the numbers wintering. Recently this species has acquired the habit of taking nuts from garden tit-feeders , even penetrating to suburban gardens.

There have been a few records suggesting that breeding may have taken place but this has not yet been confirmed.

TWITE *Carduelis flavirostris*

Very rare vagrant.

There are only three records, all recent, of this inconspicuous finch. The first was of two birds on downland near Ashmore in October 1971; the second was a single bird with a large finch flock at Swindon sewage farm December 1972; the third a party of seven on Rushall Down April 1973.

LAPLAND BUNTING *Calcarius lapponicus*

Very rare vagrant.

Only recorded once. One, possibly two, were present at Swindon sewage farm for one day in December 1953. This was a year when many were reported in the British Isles with more inland records than usual.

SNOW BUNTING *Plectrophenax nivalis*

Vagrant. Winter visitor.

A vagrant occurring rarely during the winter months. There were a number of records in the last century but only some nine in this. The more recent records were at: West Lavington January 1951; Liddington November 1959; Fyfield 1965; Roundway December 1968 into January 1969; Broad Hinton November 1975; Swindon November 1976; Bathampton Farm, Wylye, December 1978.

In addition to the species mentioned in this section there have been numerous occurrences of a variety of obvious escapes from captivity. Some of these such as Mandarin and Carolina Wood Ducks may possibly have originated in feral breeding populations but all have been excluded from this list.

A few other records have been excluded due to lack of evidence regarding their authenticity. Some other old records, such as Black Woodpecker *(Dryocopus martius)* and the Golden Winged (or Yellow-shafted) Flicker (*Colaptes auratus*) are also excluded although it appears that they would be acceptable today.

MAPS OF DISTRIBUTION

OF

BREEDING SPECIES

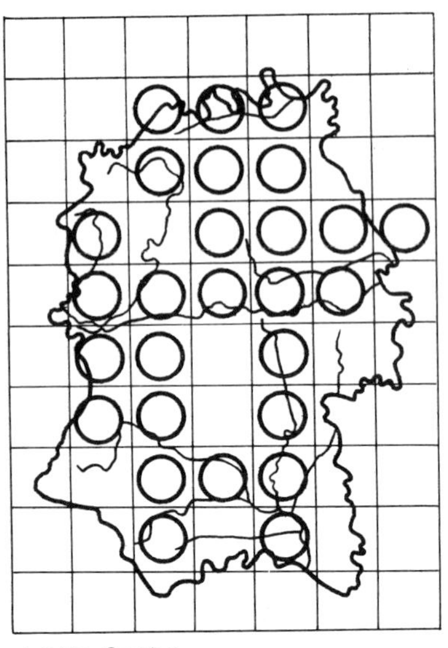
Little Grebe

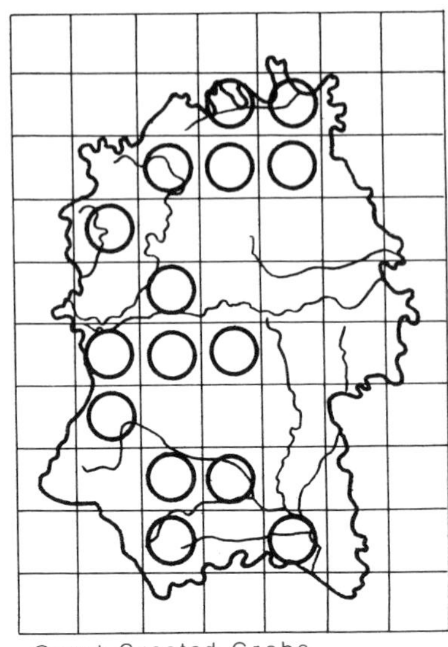
Great Crested Grebe

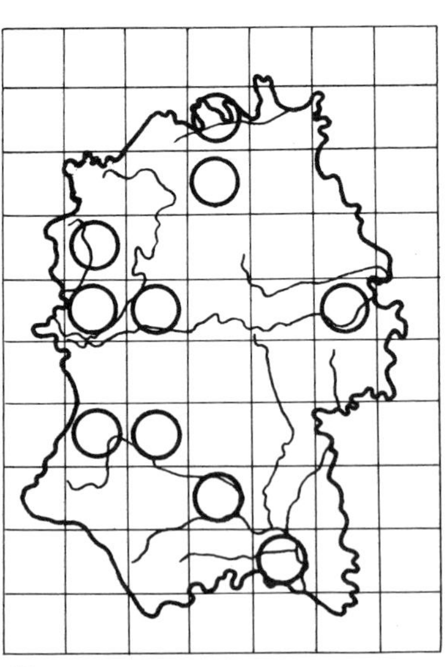
Heron

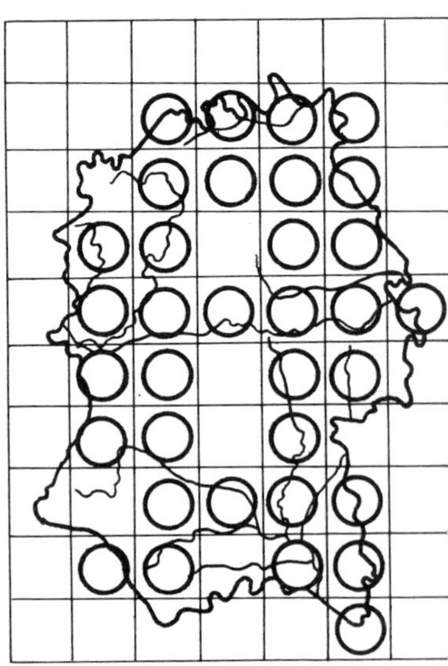
Mute Swan

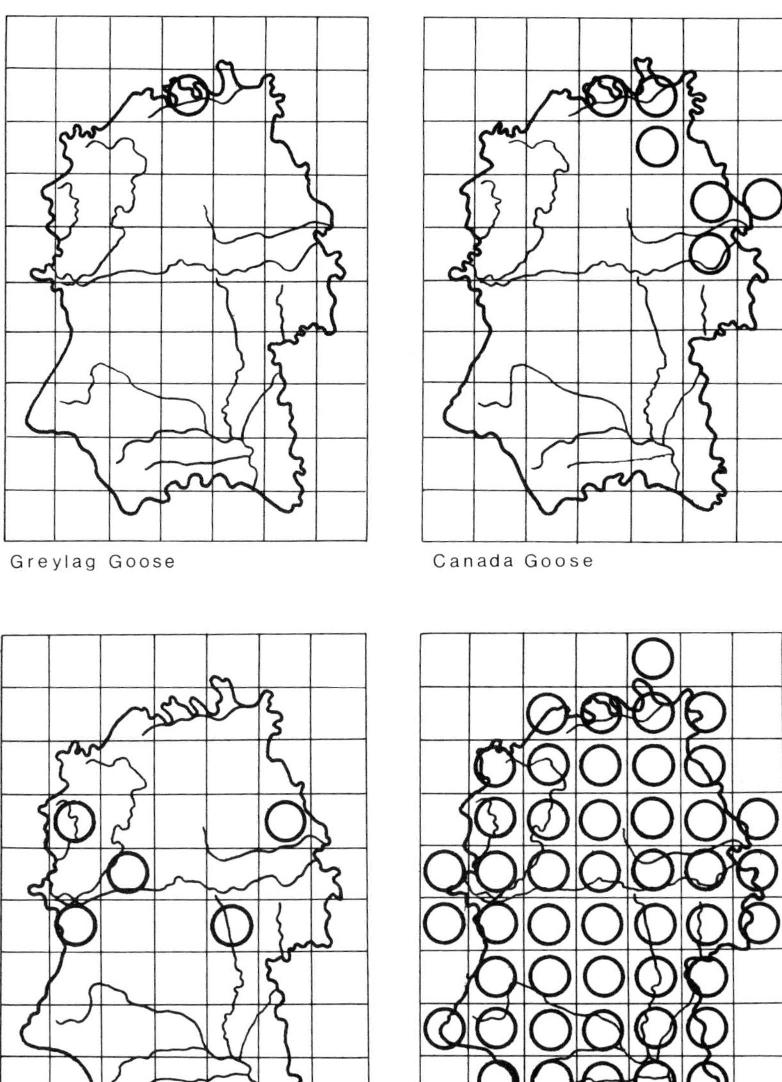

Greylag Goose

Canada Goose

Teal

Mallard

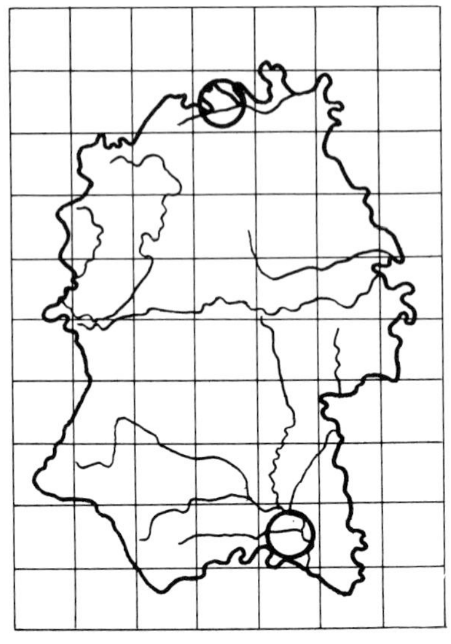

Shoveler

Red-crested Pochard

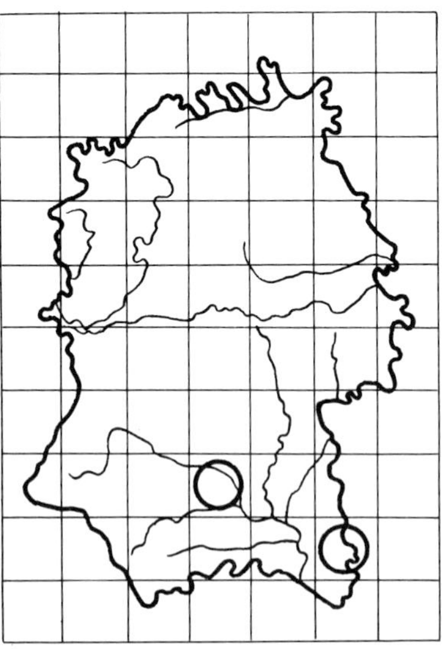

Pochard

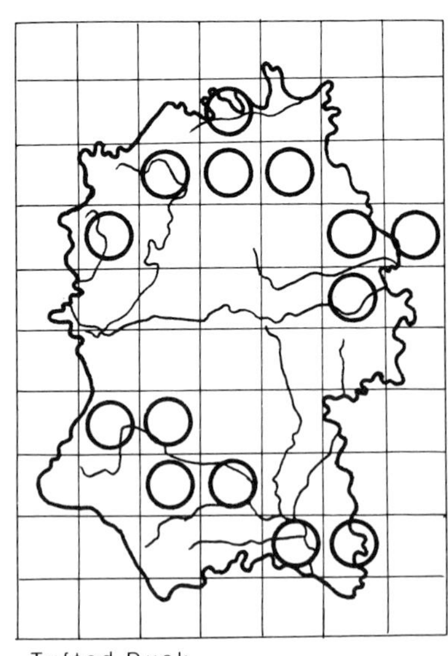

Tufted Duck

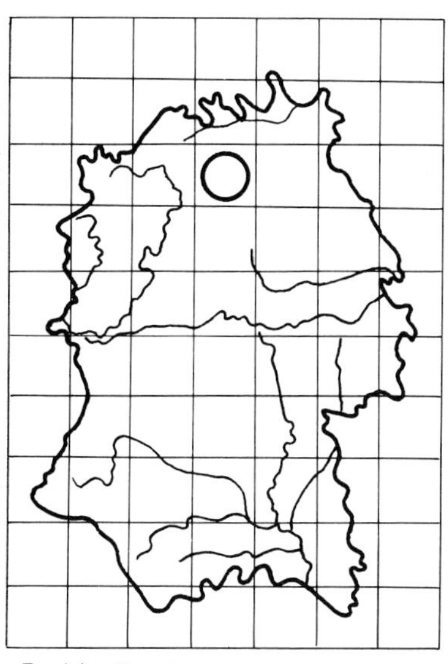

Ruddy Duck

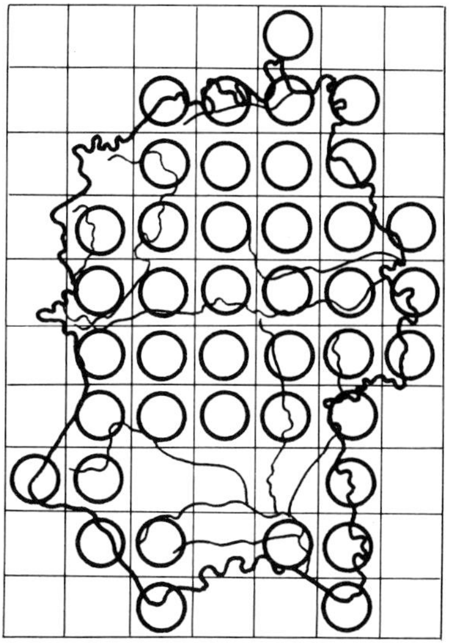

Sparrowhawk

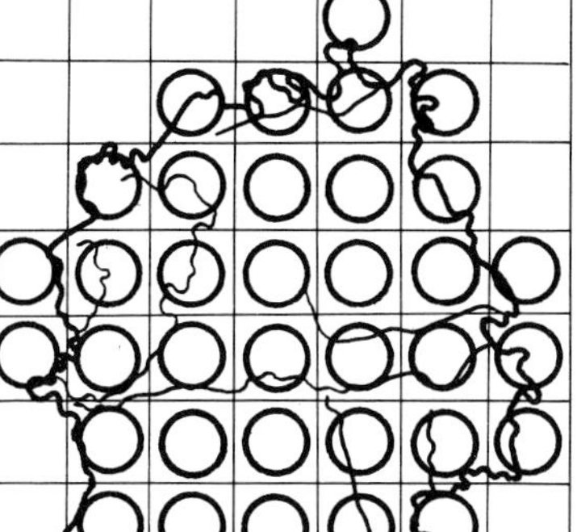

Kestrel

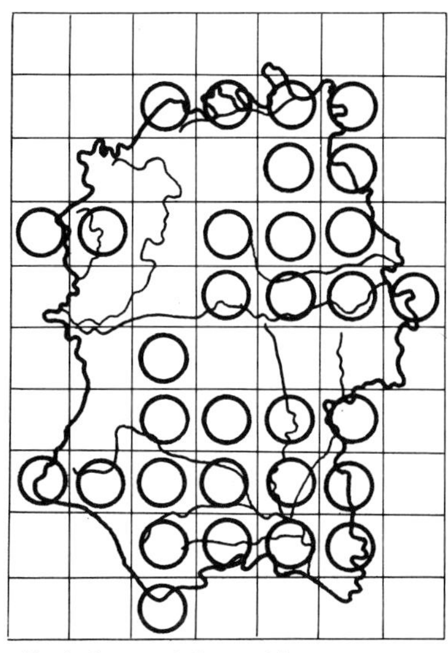

Red-legged Partridge

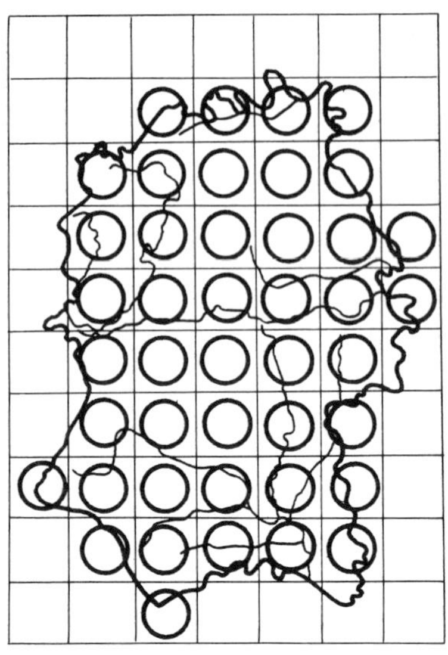

Grey Partridge

Quail

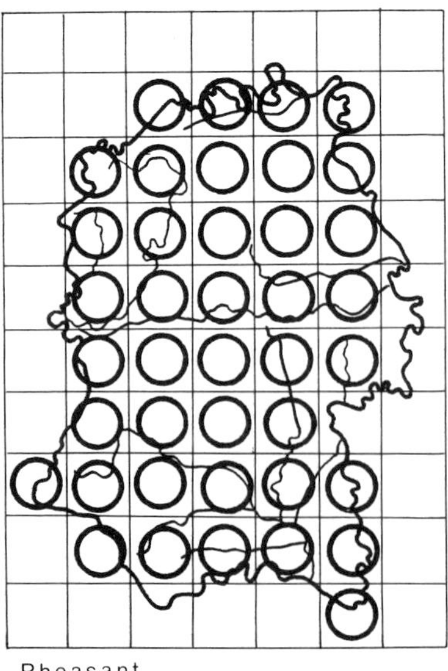

Pheasant

Moorhen

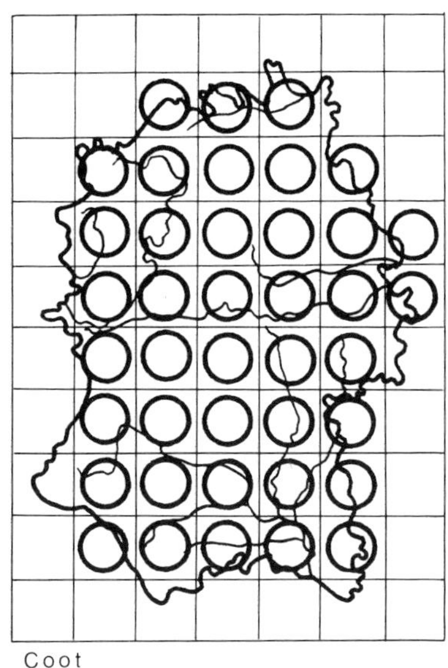
Coot

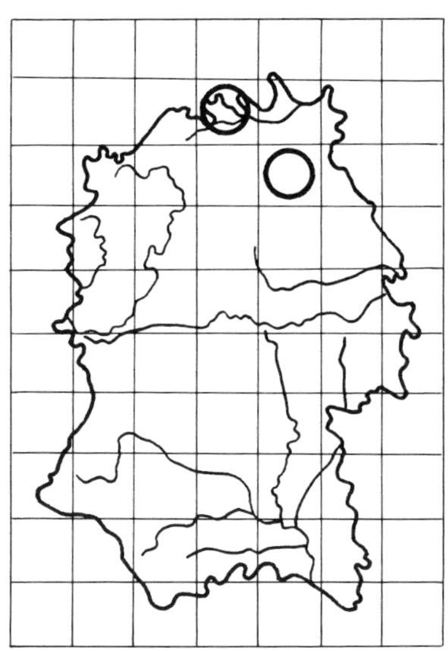
Little Ringed Plover

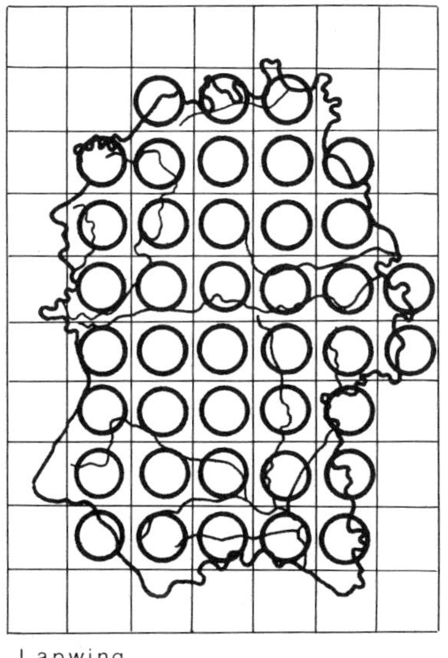
Lapwing

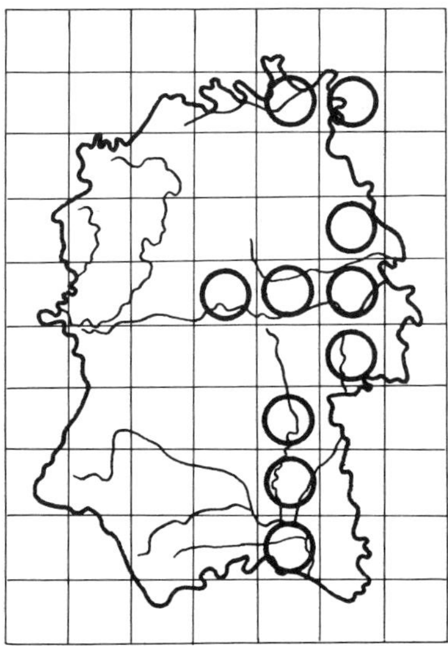
Snipe

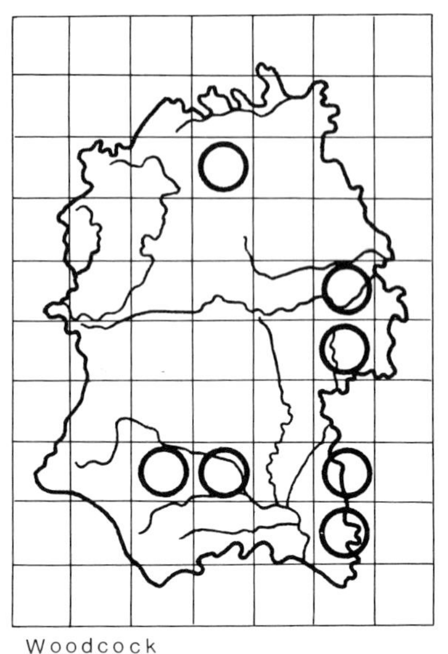
Woodcock

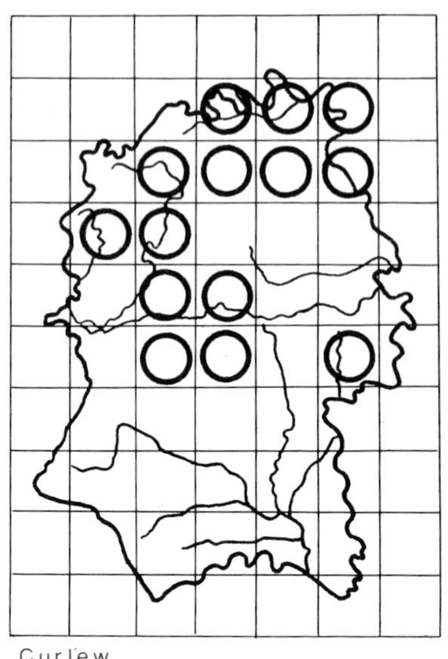
Curlew

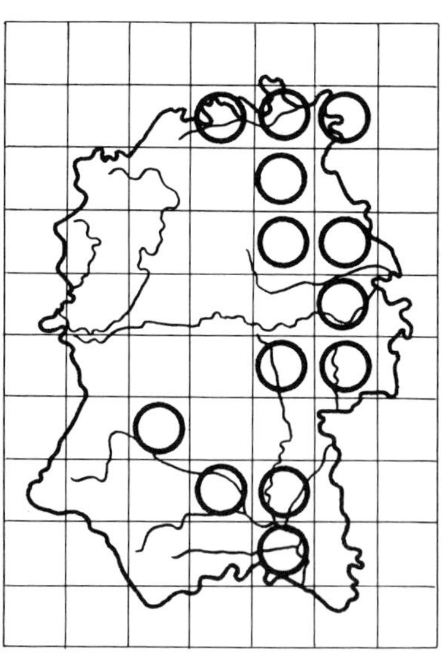
Redshank

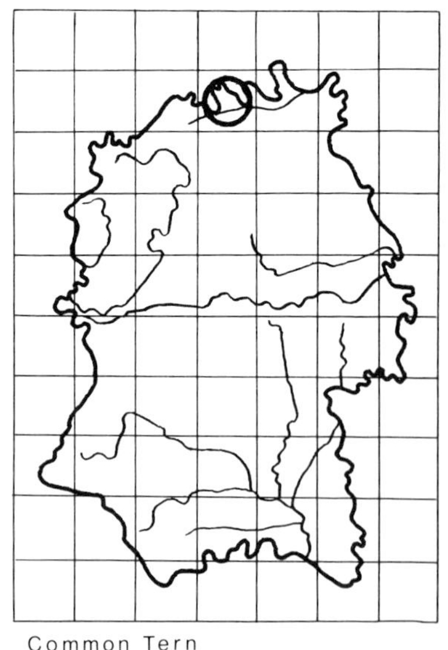
Common Tern

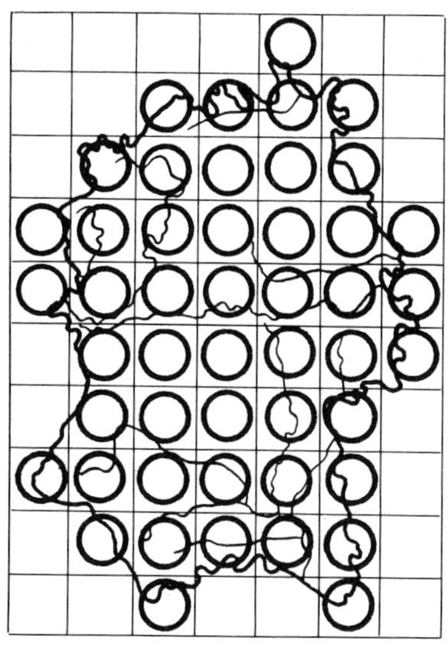

Stock Dove

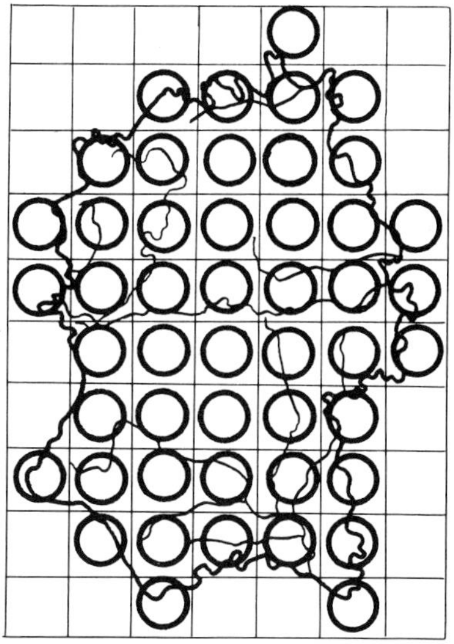

Woodpigeon

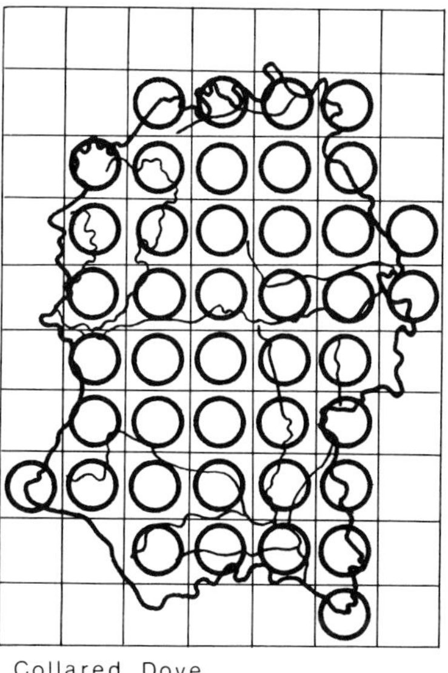

Collared Dove

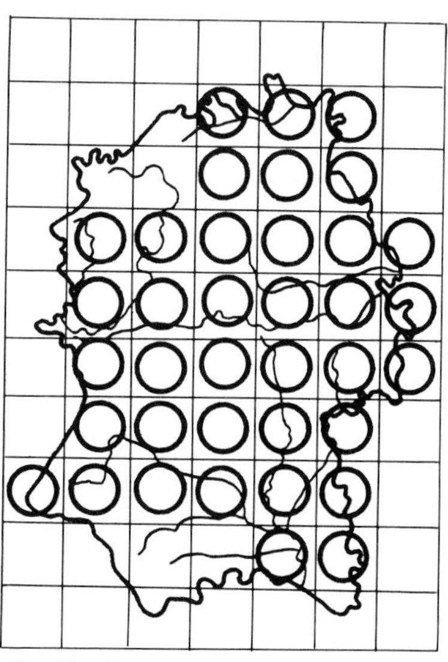

Turtle Dove

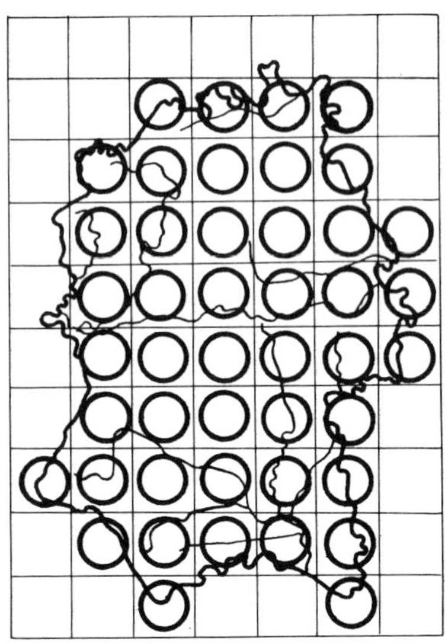

Cuckoo

Barn Owl

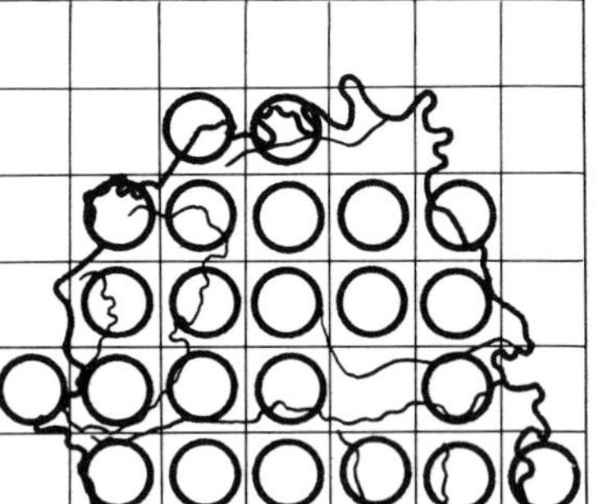

Little Owl

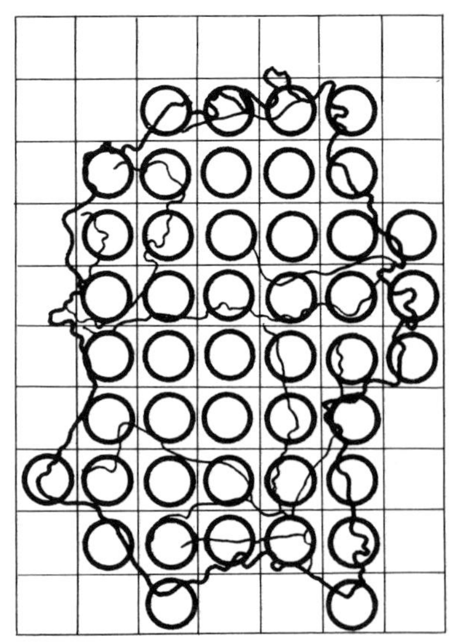

Tawny Owl

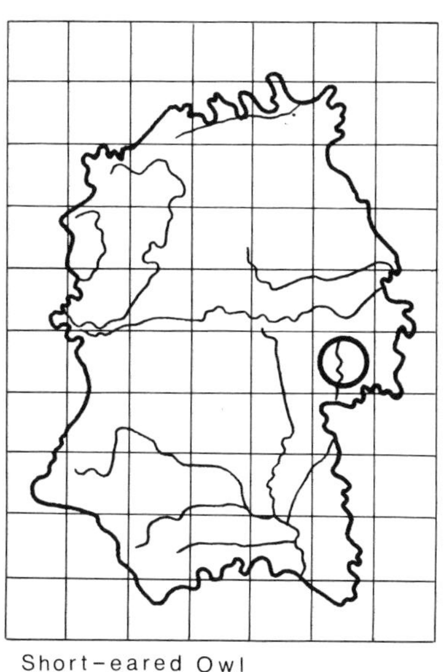
Short-eared Owl

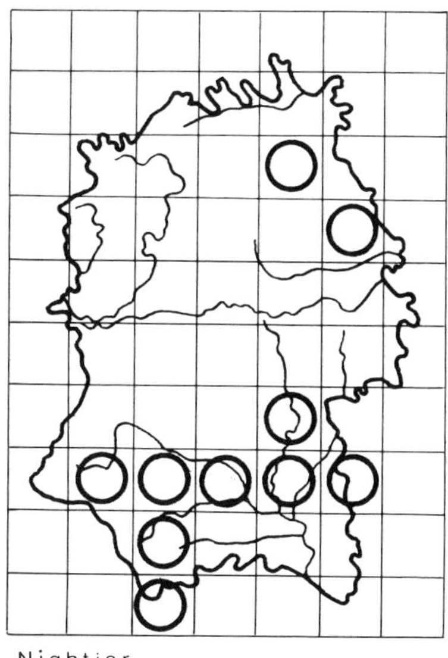
Nightjar

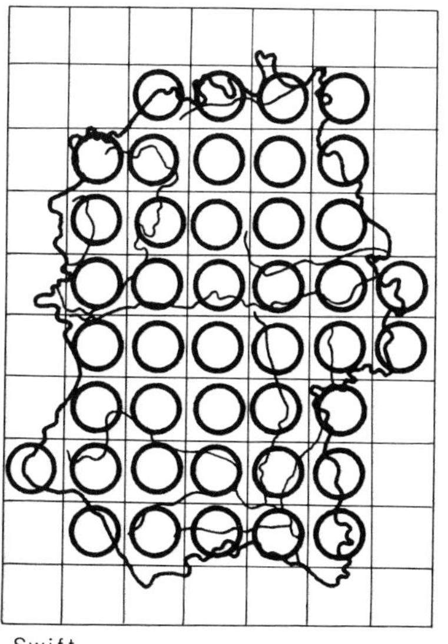
Swift

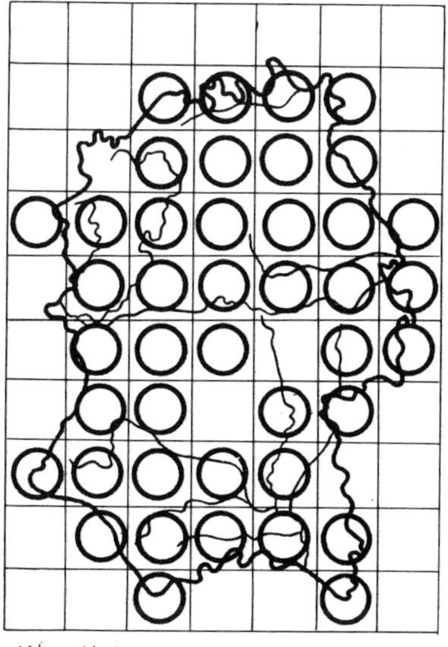
Kingfisher

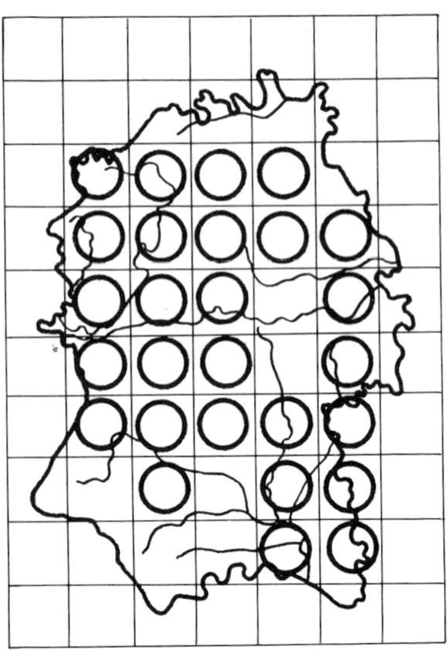

Green Woodpecker

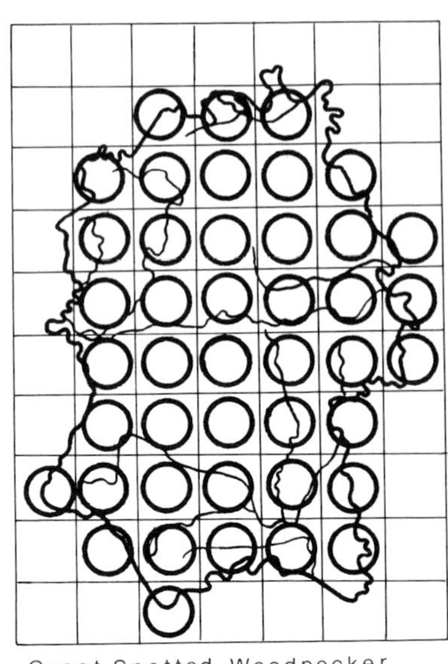

Great Spotted Woodpecker

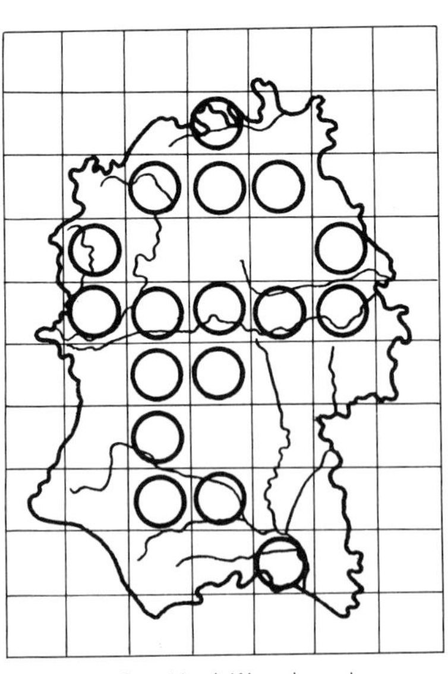

Lesser Spotted Woodpecker

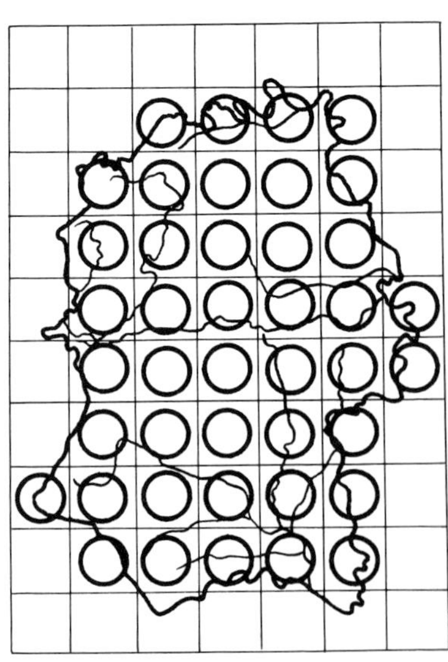

Skylark

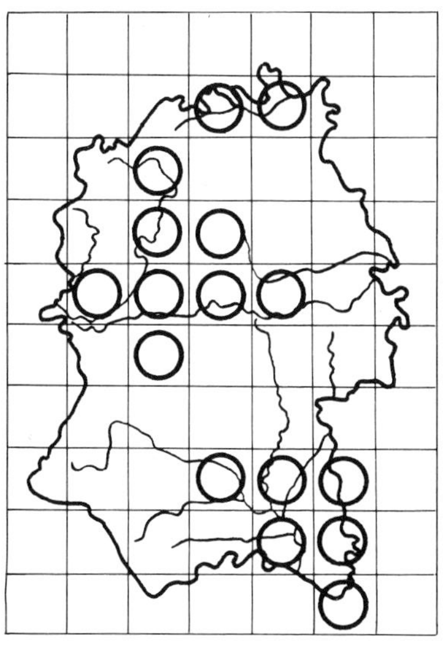

Sand Martin

Swallow

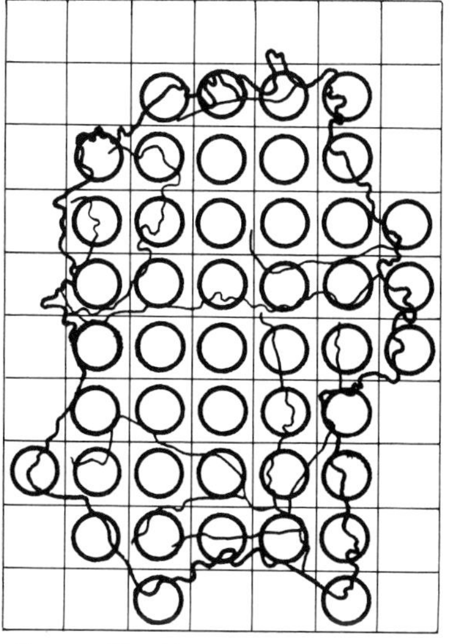

House Martin

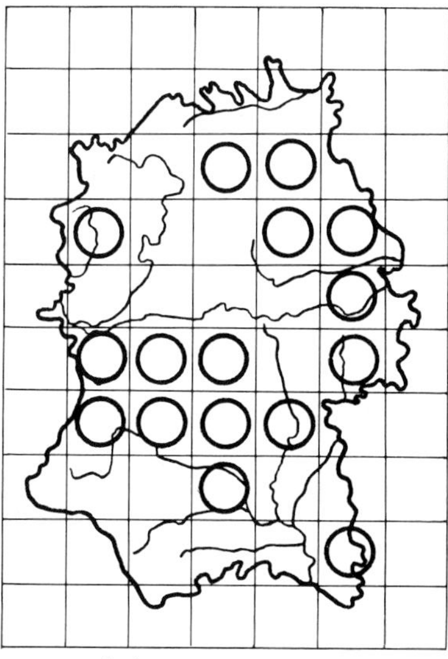

Tree Pipit

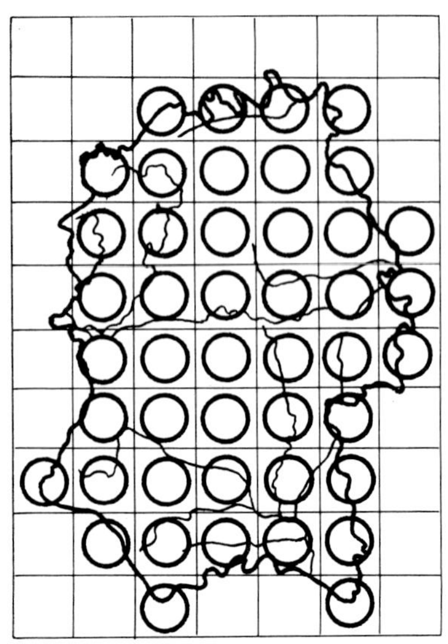

Meadow Pipit

Yellow Wagtail

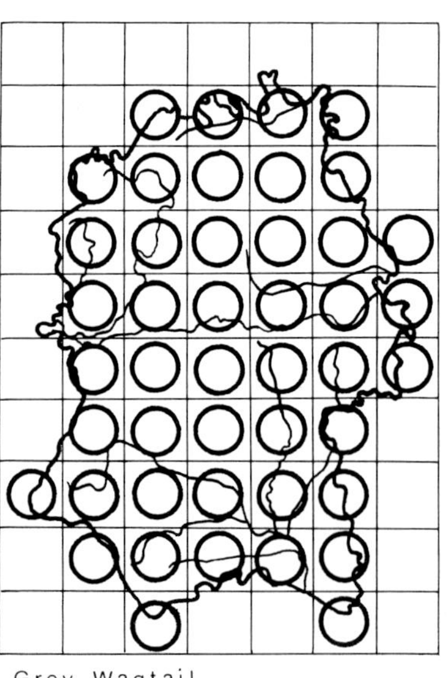

Grey Wagtail

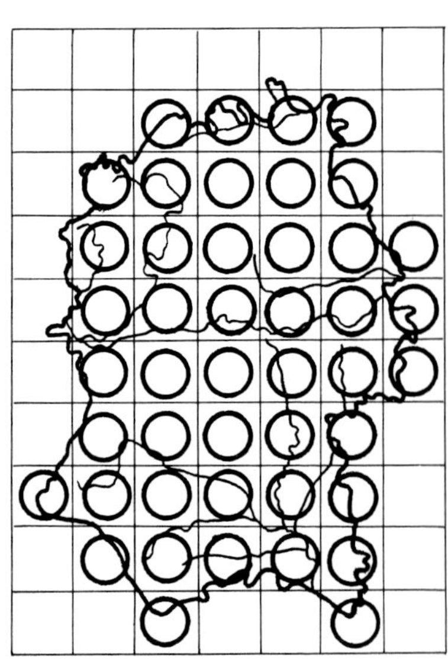

Pied Wagtail

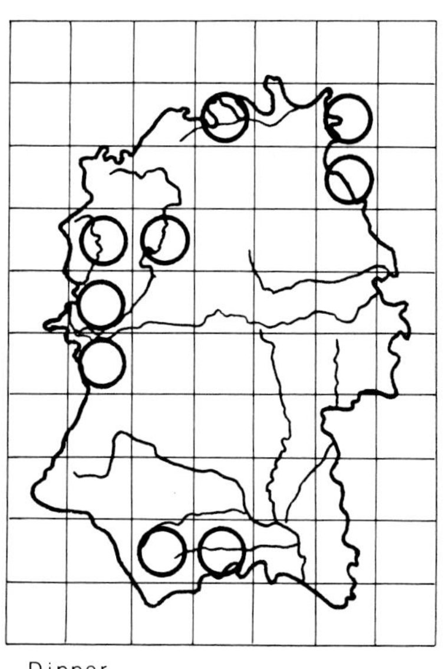

Dipper

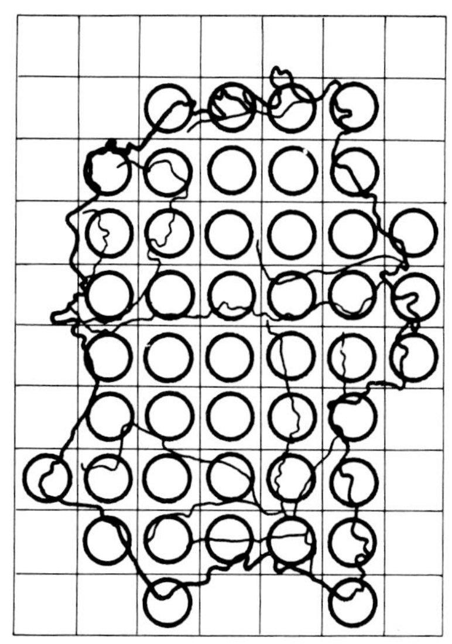

Wren

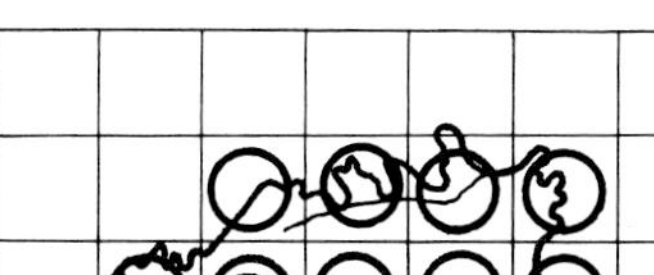

Dunnock

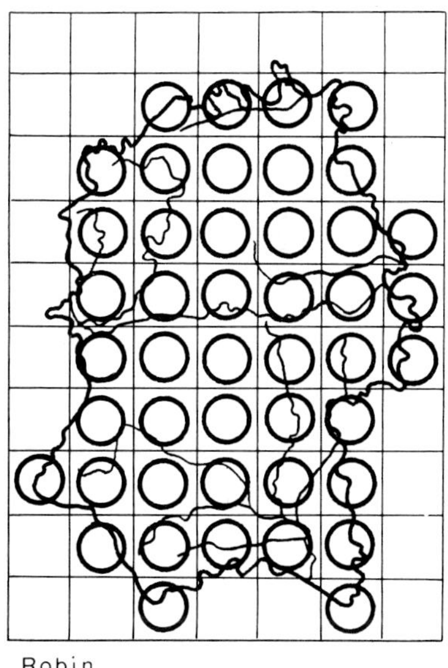

Robin

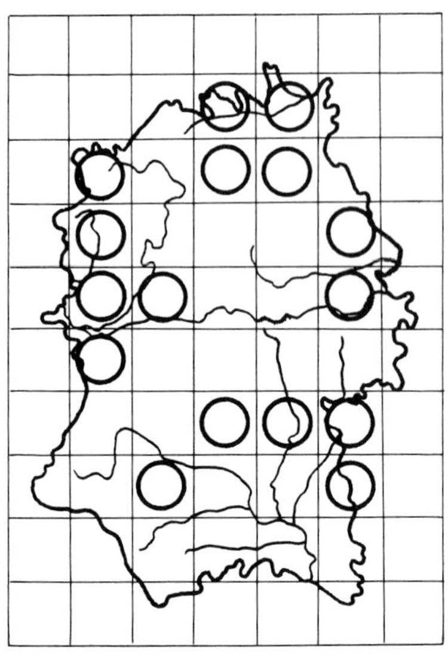
Nightingale

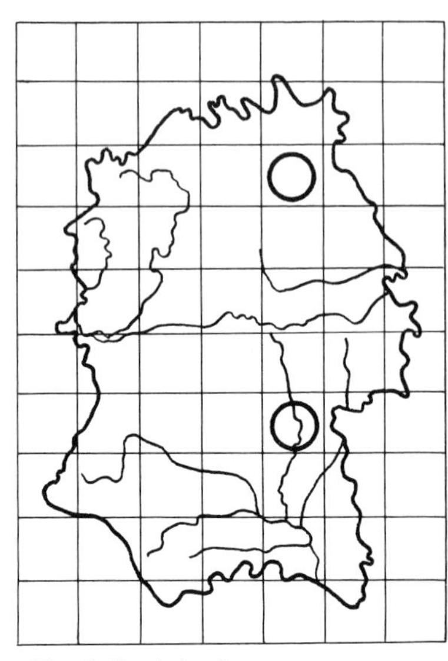
Black Redstart

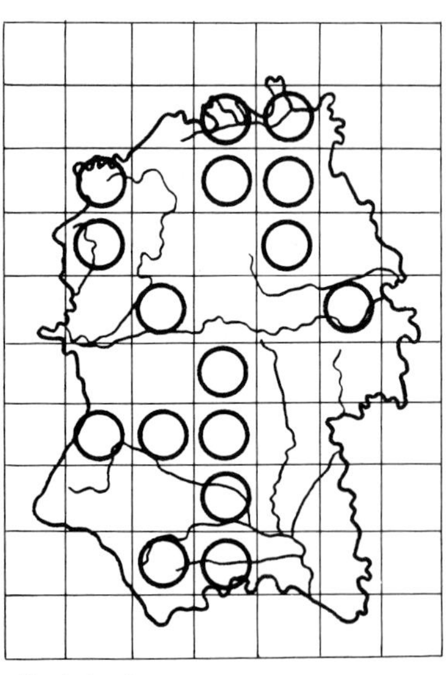
Redstart

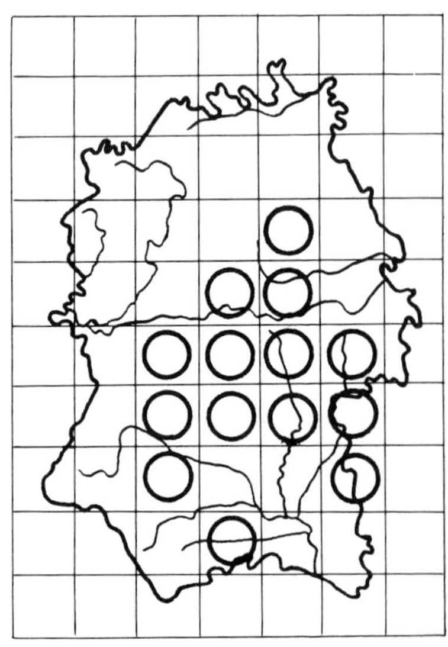
Whinchat

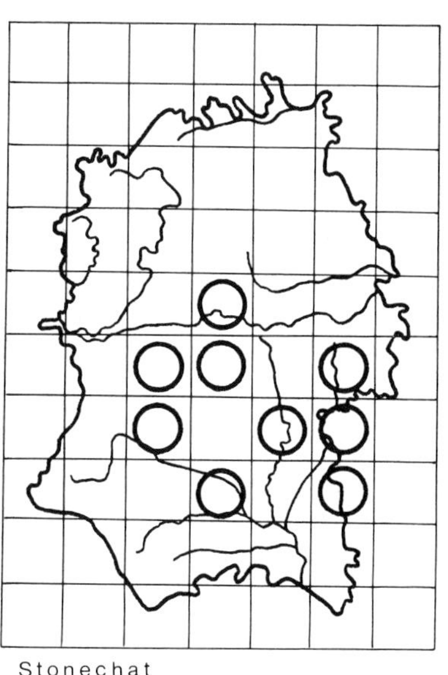

Stonechat

Wheatear

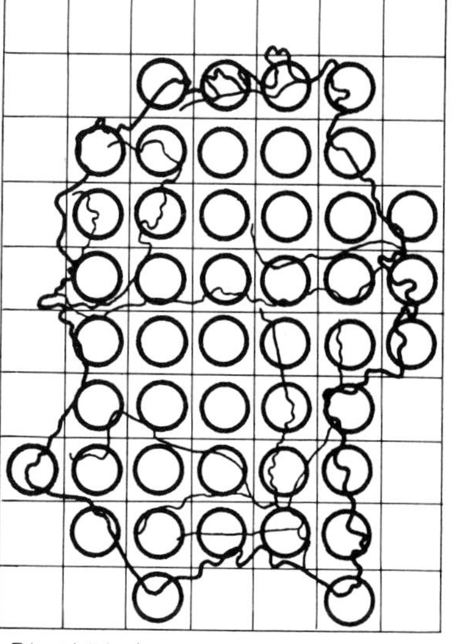

Blackbird

Song Thrush

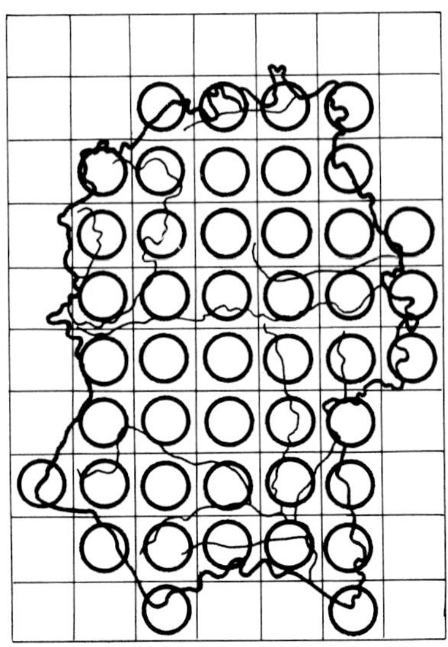
Mistle Thrush

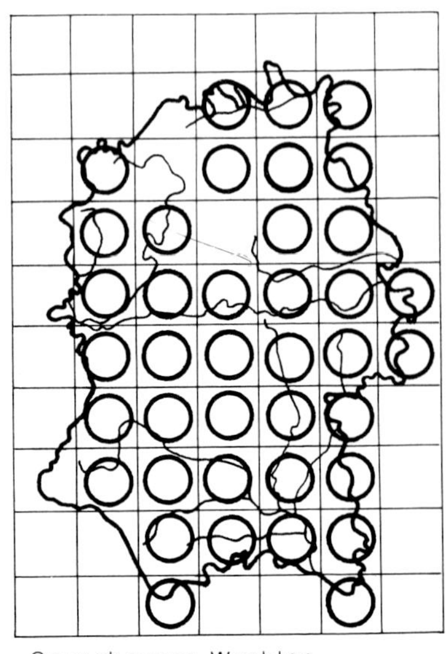
Grasshopper Warbler

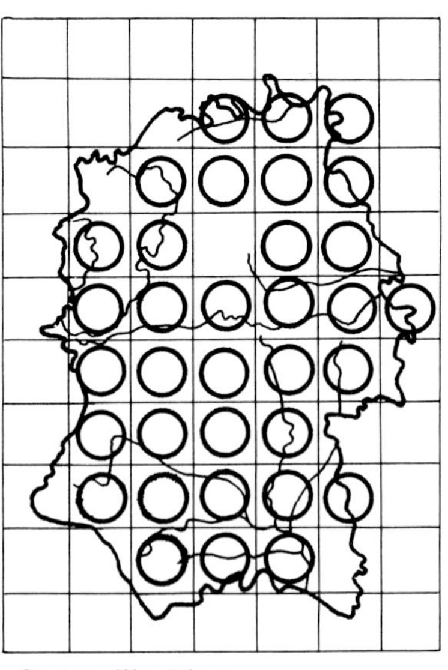
Sedge Warbler

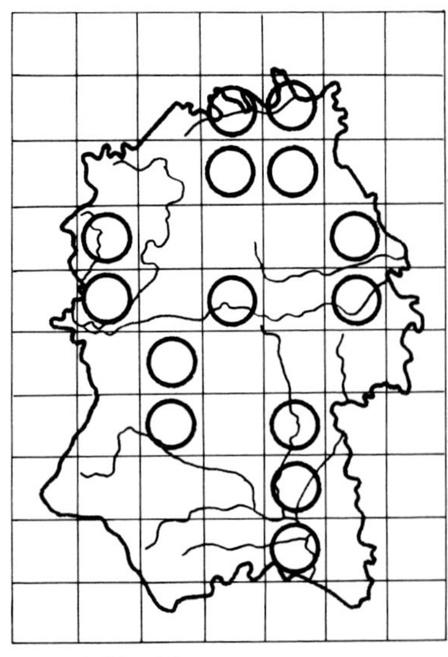
Reed Warbler

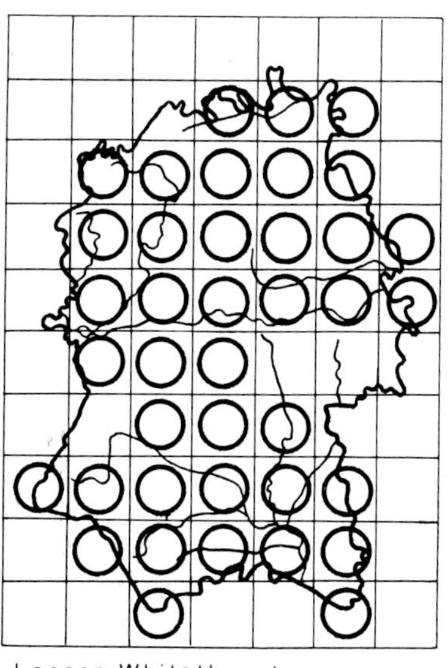
Lesser Whitethroat

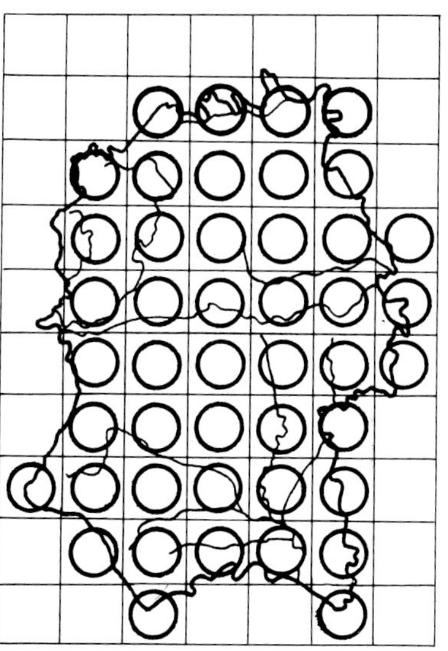
Whitethroat

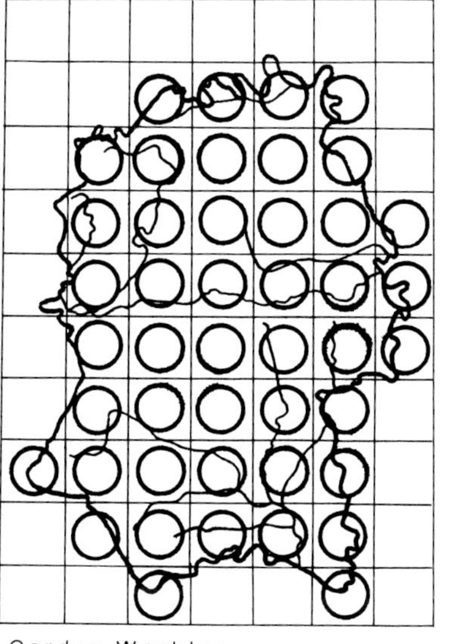
Garden Warbler

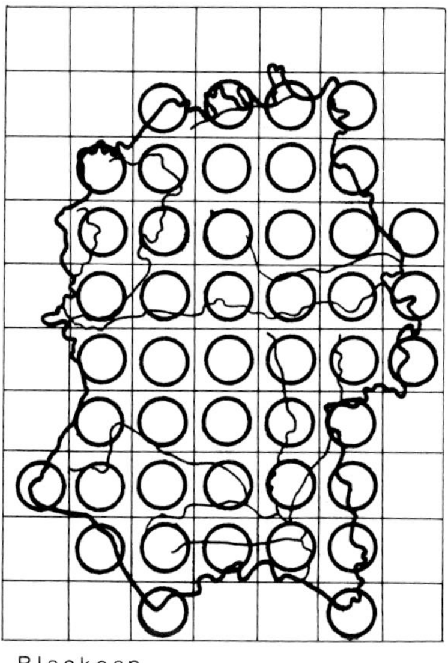
Blackcap

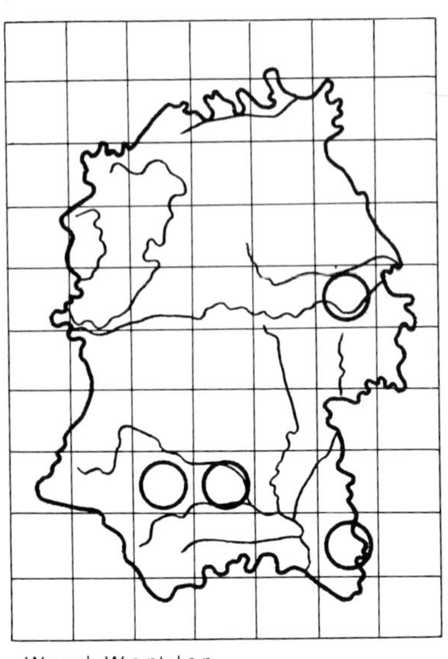

Wood Warbler

Chiffchaff

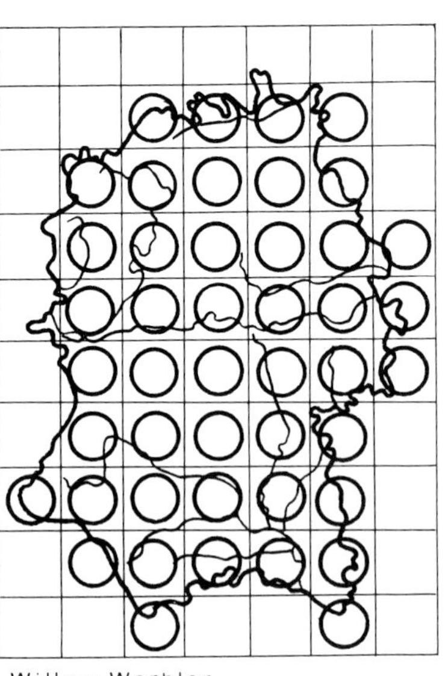

Willow Warbler

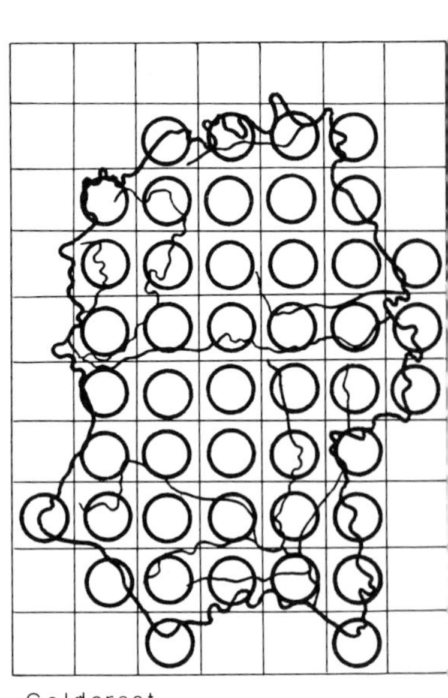

Goldcrest

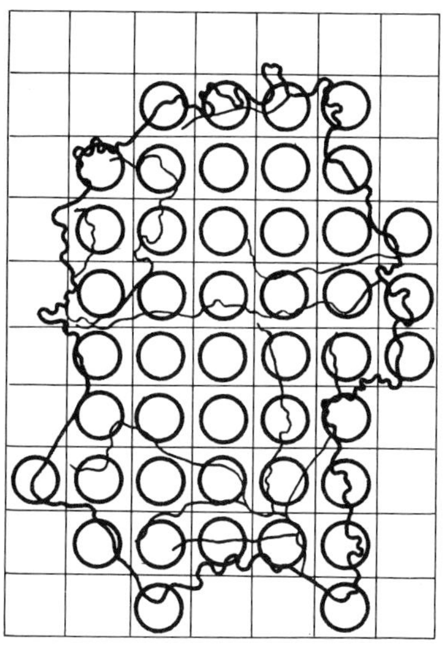

Spotted Flycatcher

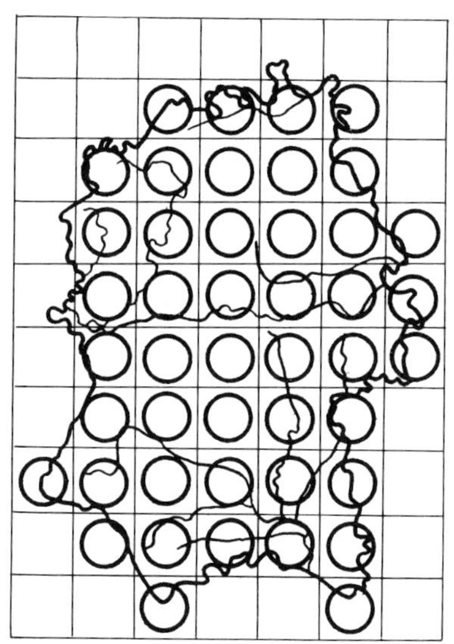

Long-tailed Tit

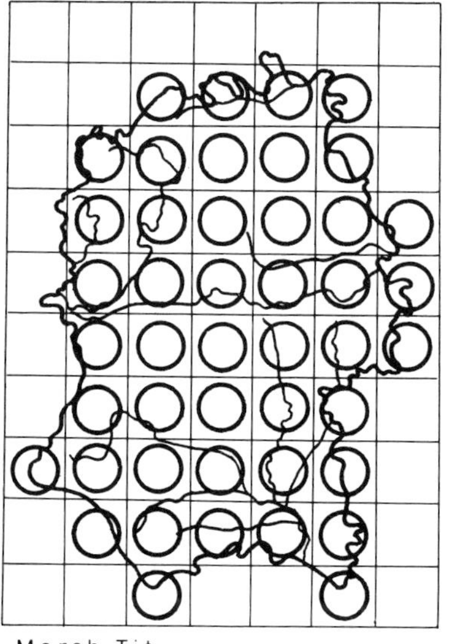

Marsh Tit

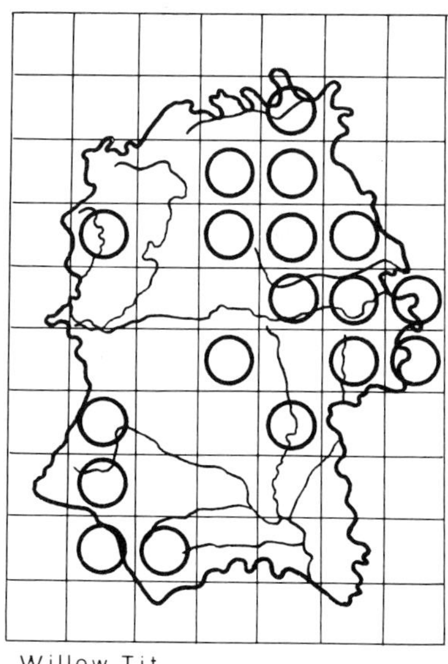

Willow Tit

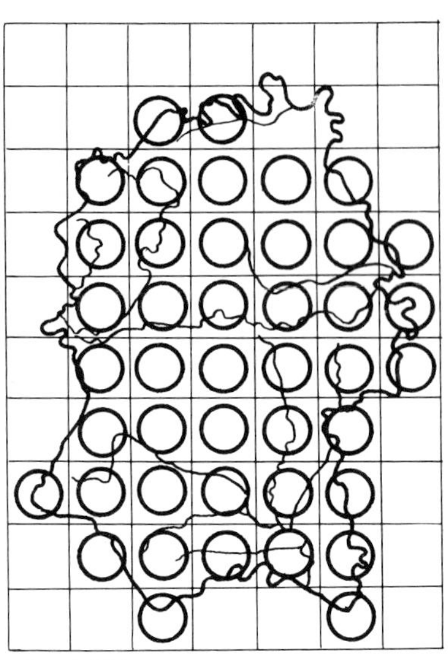
Coal Tit

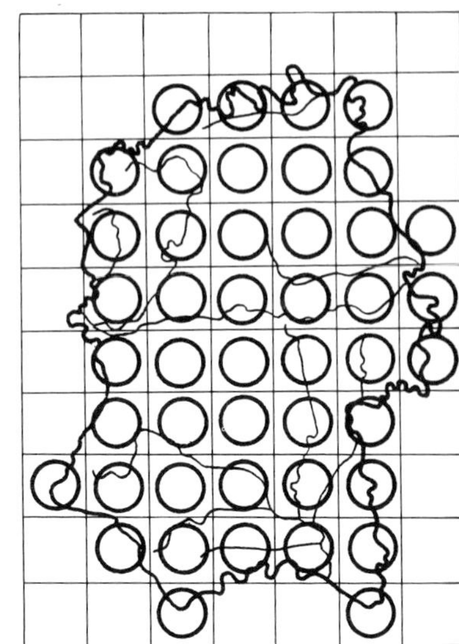
Blue Tit

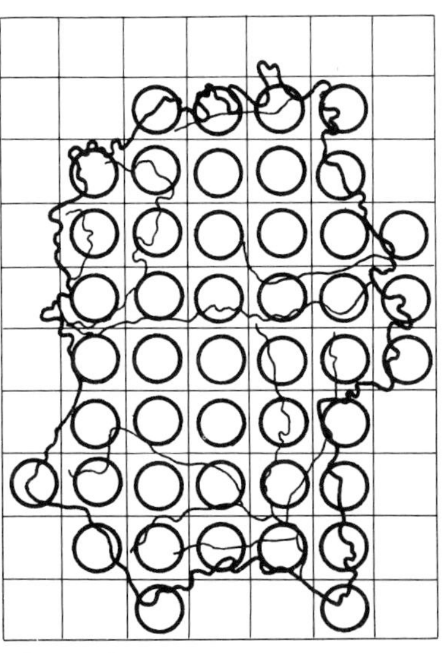
Great Tit

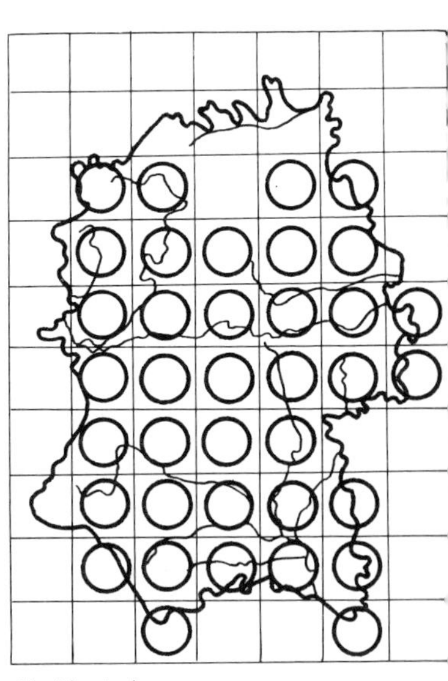
Nuthatch

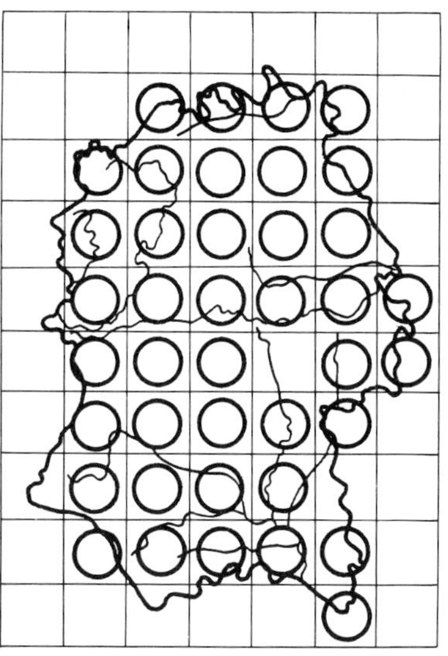

Treecreeper

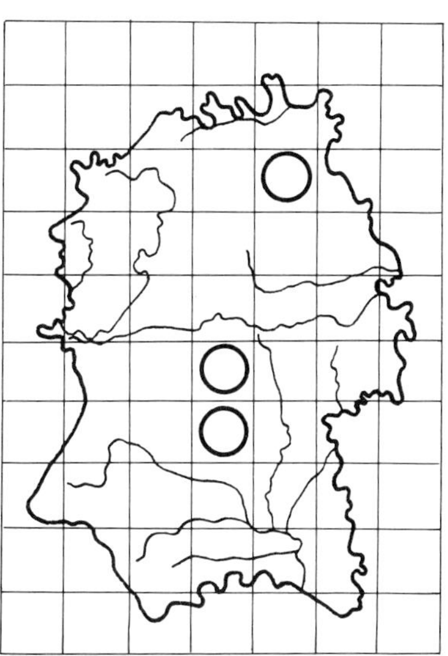

Red-backed Shrike

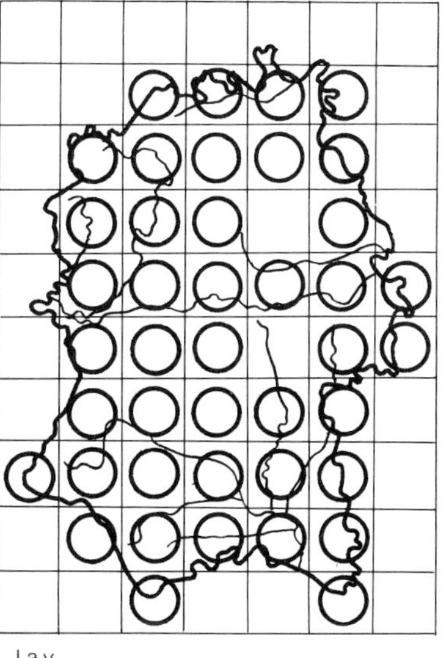

Jay

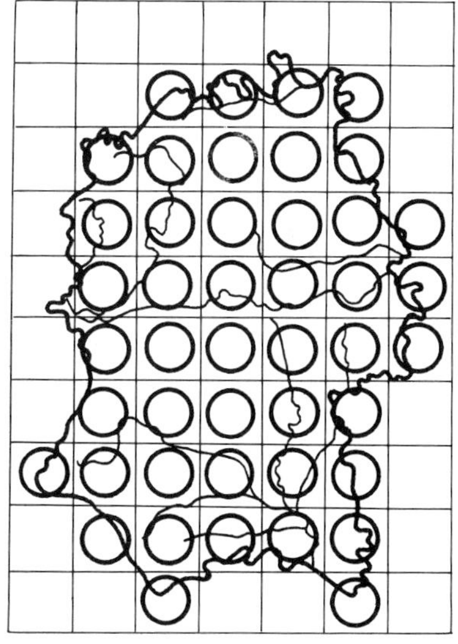

Magpie

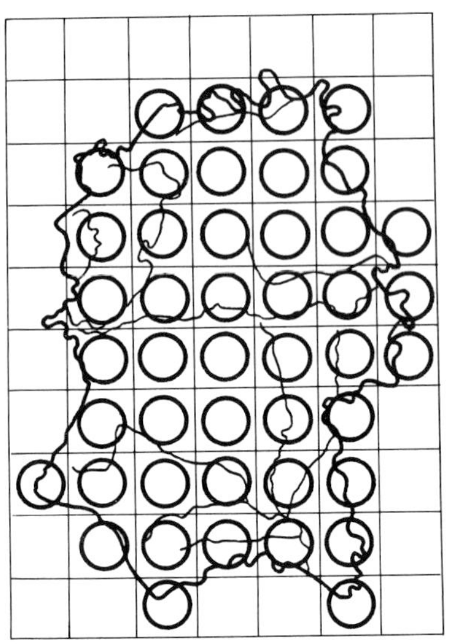
Jackdaw

Rook

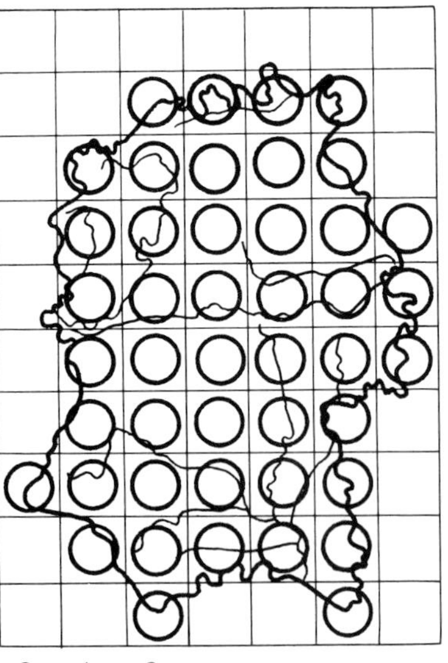
Carrion Crow

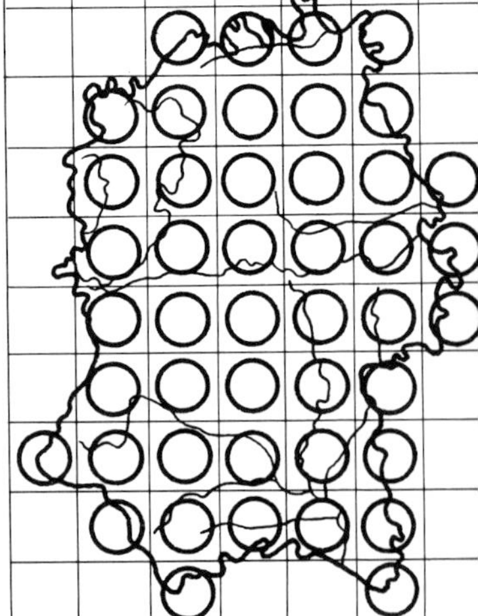
Starling

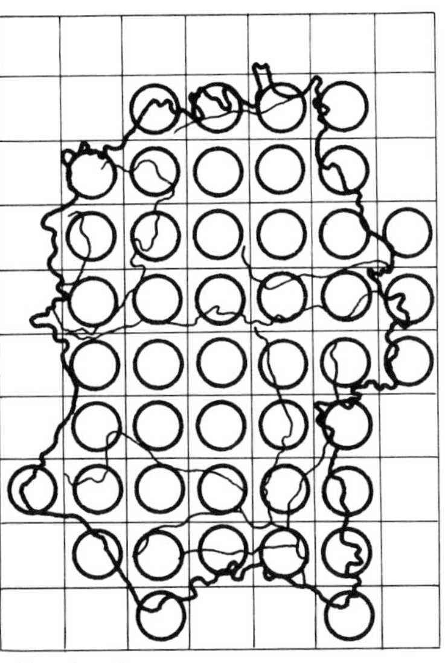
House Sparrow

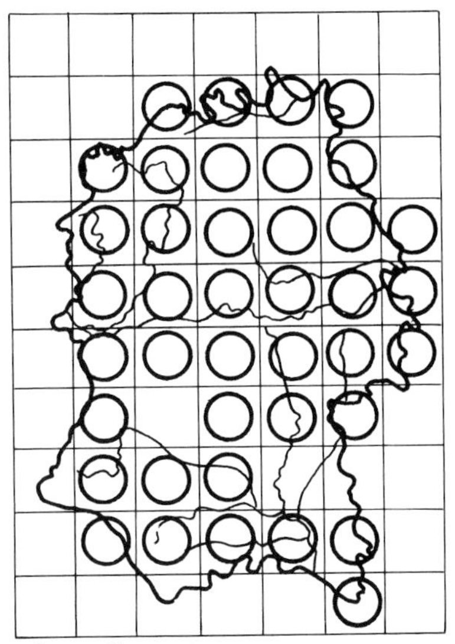
Tree Sparrow

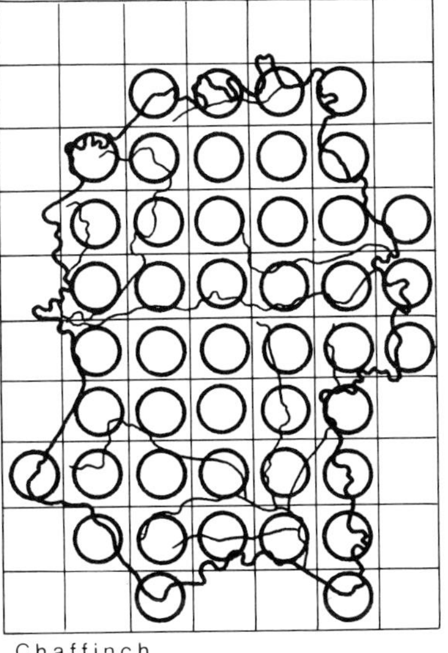
Chaffinch

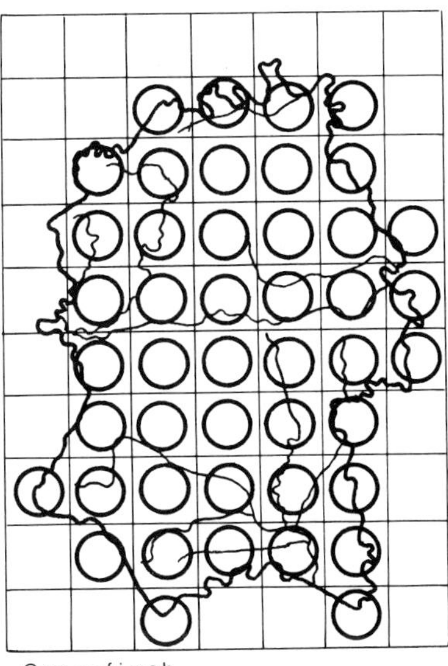
Greenfinch

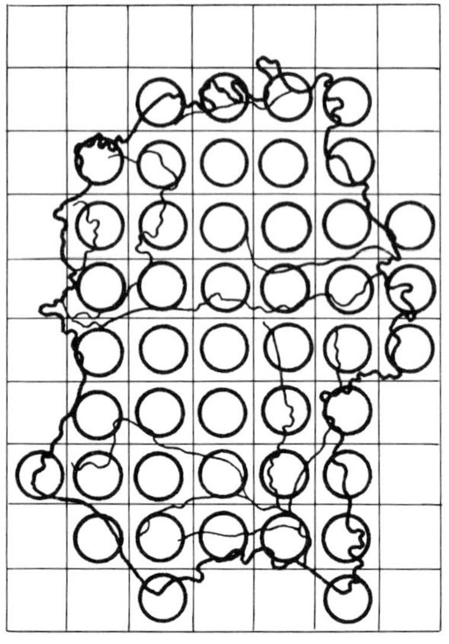

Goldfinch

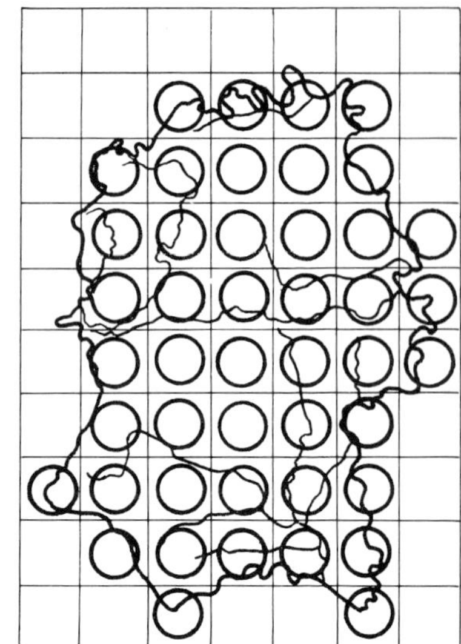

Linnet

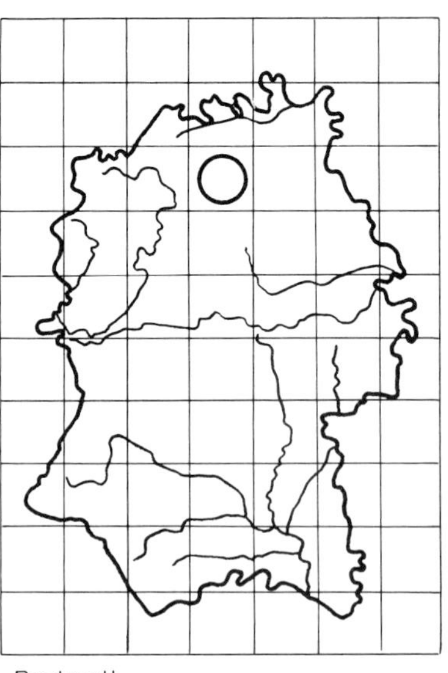

Redpoll

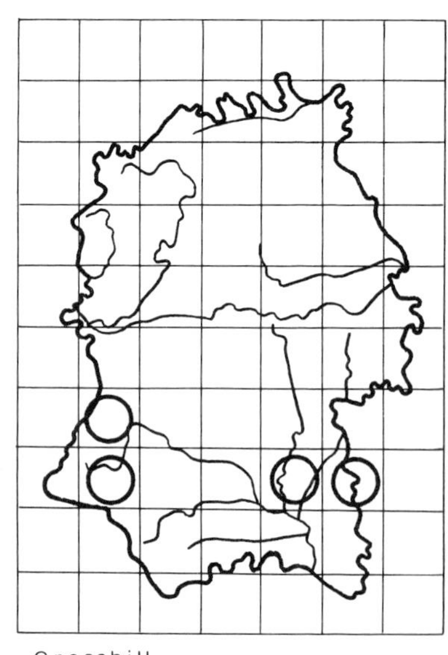

Crossbill

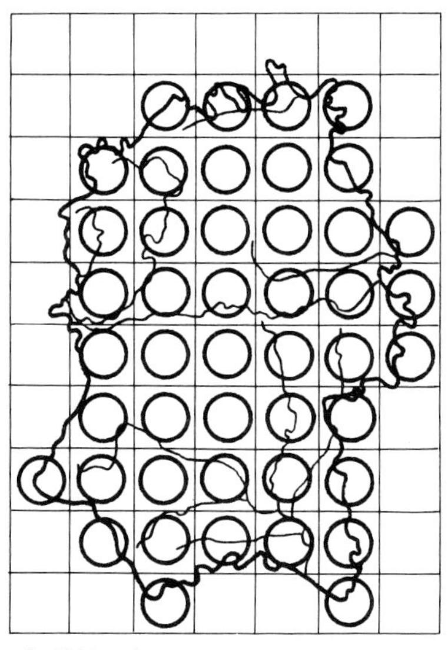

Bullfinch

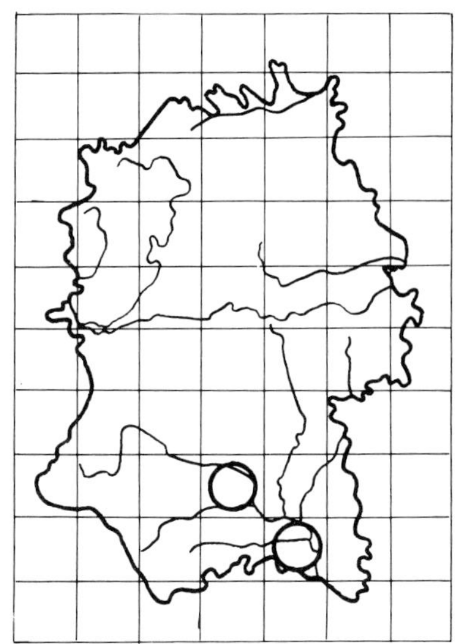

Hawfinch

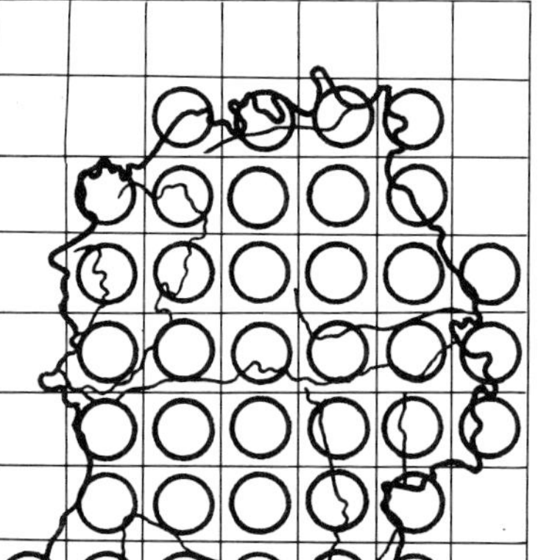

Yellowhammer

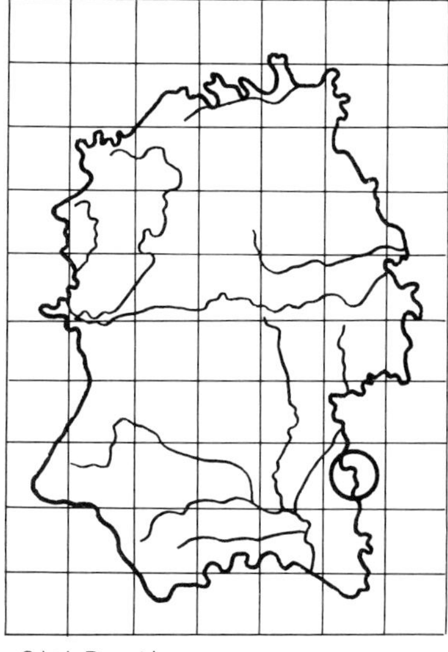

Cirl Bunting

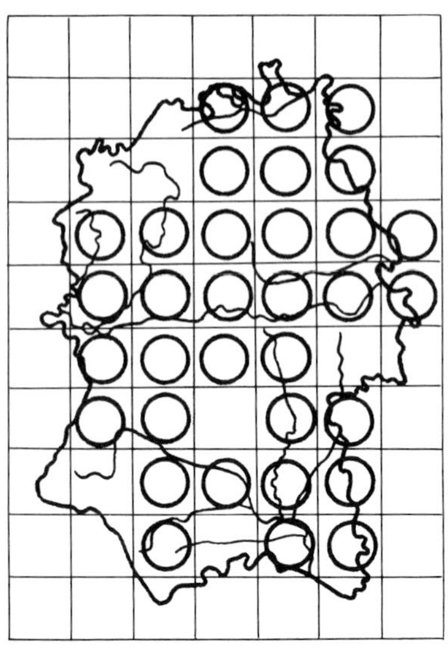

Reed Bunting

Corn Bunting

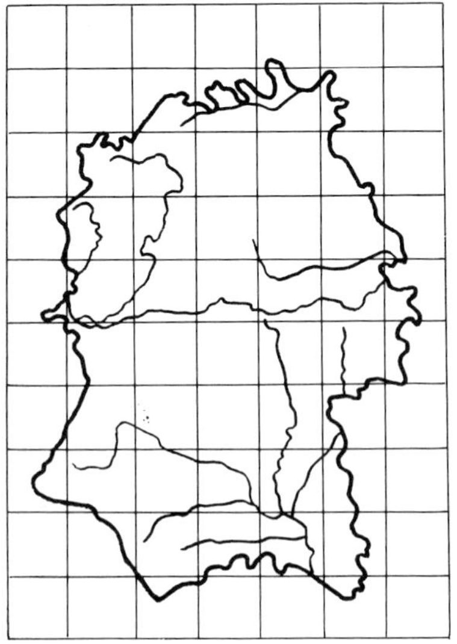

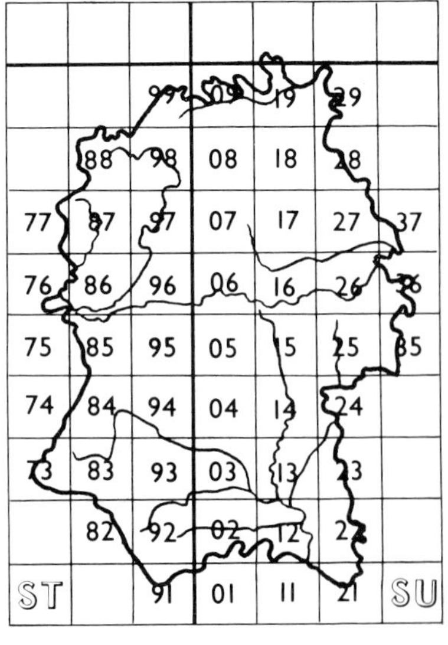

BIBLIOGRAPHY

Alexander, W.B.: The Woodcock in the British Isles. (Reprinted from *Ibis*, 87-89) 1947-49.

Aubrey, John: The Natural History of Wiltshire, ed. John Britton, 1847.

Barron, E.S.: The Geology of Wiltshire, Bradford-on-Avon, 1976.

Chafin, W.: Anecdotes and History of Cranborne Chase. 1818.

Gillam, B.: Checklists of the Birds of the Imber Ranges. 1974, 1977.

Gover, J.E.B., Allen Mawer and F.M. Stenton: The Place-Names of Wiltshire. (English Place-Name Society, vol. XVI.) Cambridge, 1939.

Grose, Donald: The Flora of Wiltshire. Devizes, 1957.

Halliday, J.H. and H.T. Randolph: Handlist of the Birds of the Marlborough District. 1955.

Hoare, Sir Richard Colt: Ancient History of Wiltshire, 1810-19.

Im Thurn, Everard: The Birds of Marlborough. 1870.

Irwin, Raymond: British Birds and their Books. Cambridge, 1952.

Jefferies, Richard: Wild Life in a Southern County. 1879.

Maton, W.G.: Natural History of part of the County of Wiltshire. 1843.

Paris, J.A.: A Biographical Sketch of the late William George Maton. 1838.

Peirson, L.G.: Handlist of the Birds of the Marlborough District. 1939.

: Wiltshire Birds. Devizes, 1959.

Prendergast, E.D.V.: Checklist of the Birds of the Larkhill Artillery Ranges. 1971.

Ratcliffe, Derek: The Peregrine Falcon, Calton, 1980.

Sharrock, J.T.R.: The Atlas of Breeding Birds in Britain and Ireland. Tring, 1976.

Smith, A.C.: The Birds of Wiltshire. 1887.

Snow, D.W. (Ed.): The Status of Birds in Britain and Ireland. Oxford, 1971.

Southwood, T.R.E.: The number of species of insect associated with various trees. *Journal of Animal Ecology*, 30. 1961.

Stearn, L.F. (Ed.): Supplement to the Flora of Wiltshire. Devizes. 1975.

Thomas, H.: Salisbury Plain. 1976.

Voous, K.H.: List of Recent Holarctic Bird Species. 1977.

Webber, G.L.: Supplement to *Wiltshire Birds*. Trowbridge. 1967.

Whitlock, R.: Salisbury Plain. 1955.

Witherby, H.F., F.C.R. Jourdain, N.F. Ticehurst and B.W. Tucker: The Handbook of British Birds. 1938-41.

The following journals have been invaluable:

Bird Study
British Birds
The Field
Hobby
Ibis
Journal of Animal Ecology
Wiltshire Archaeological and Natural History Magazine
Wiltshire Notes and Queries
The Zoologist

Manuscript sources include:

Bowood Estate Game Books
Longford Castle Game Books
Notes by Rev. George Marsh in his interleaved copy of Yarrell's History of British Birds, in the British Museum (Natural History) at Tring.
Papers of Rev. Arthur P. Morres.

INDEX

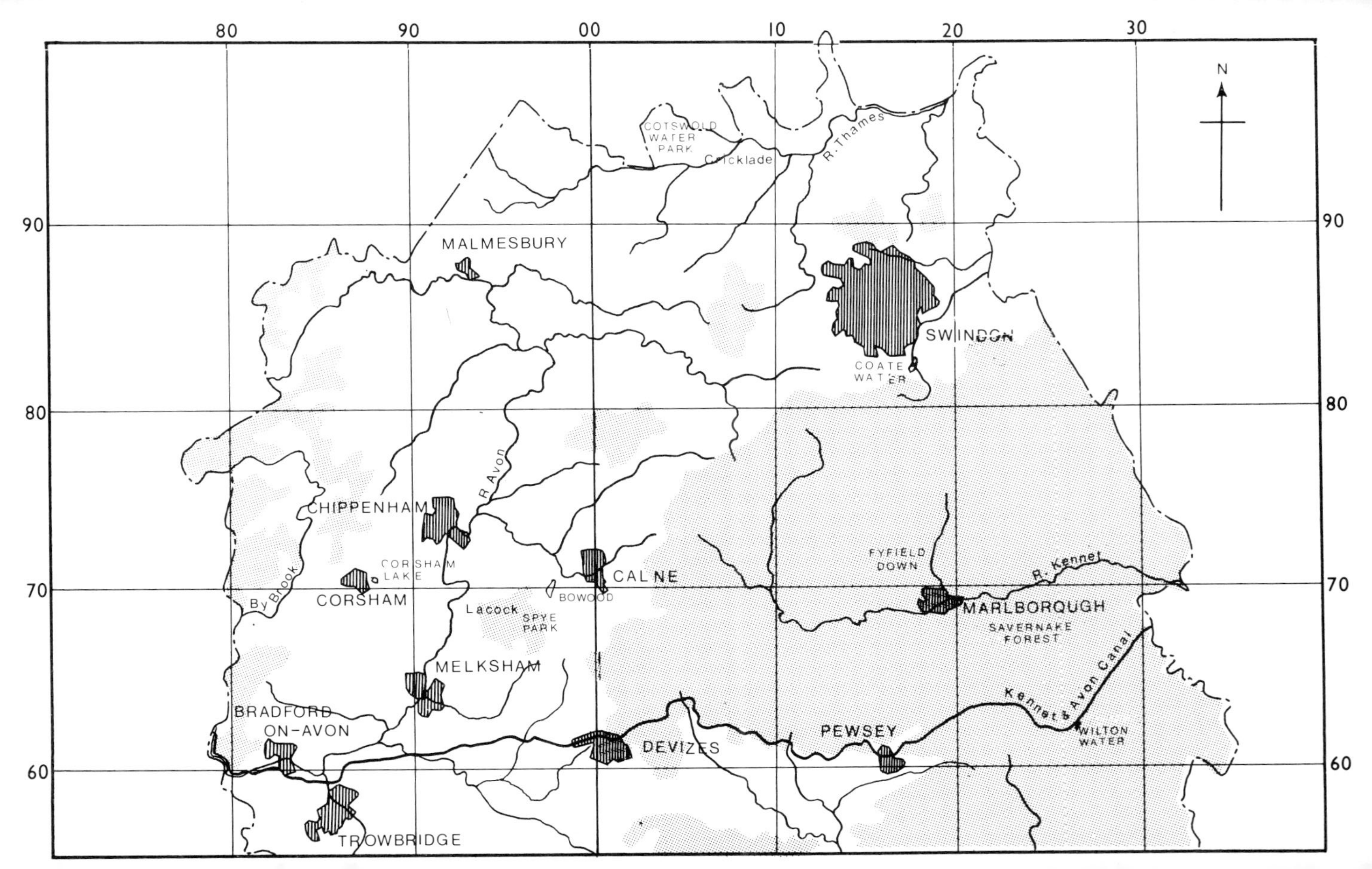

80
90
00
10
20
30
N
COTSWOLD WATER PARK
Cricklade
R. Thames
MALMESBURY
SWINDON
COATE WATER
CHIPPENHAM
R Avon
CORSHAM LAKE
CORSHAM
By Brook
CALNE
BOWOOD
Lacock
SPYE PARK
FYFIELD DOWN
R. Kennet
MARLBOROUGH
SAVERNAKE FOREST
MELKSHAM
BRADFORD ON-AVON
DEVIZES
PEWSEY
Kennet & Avon Canal
WILTON WATER
TROWBRIDGE

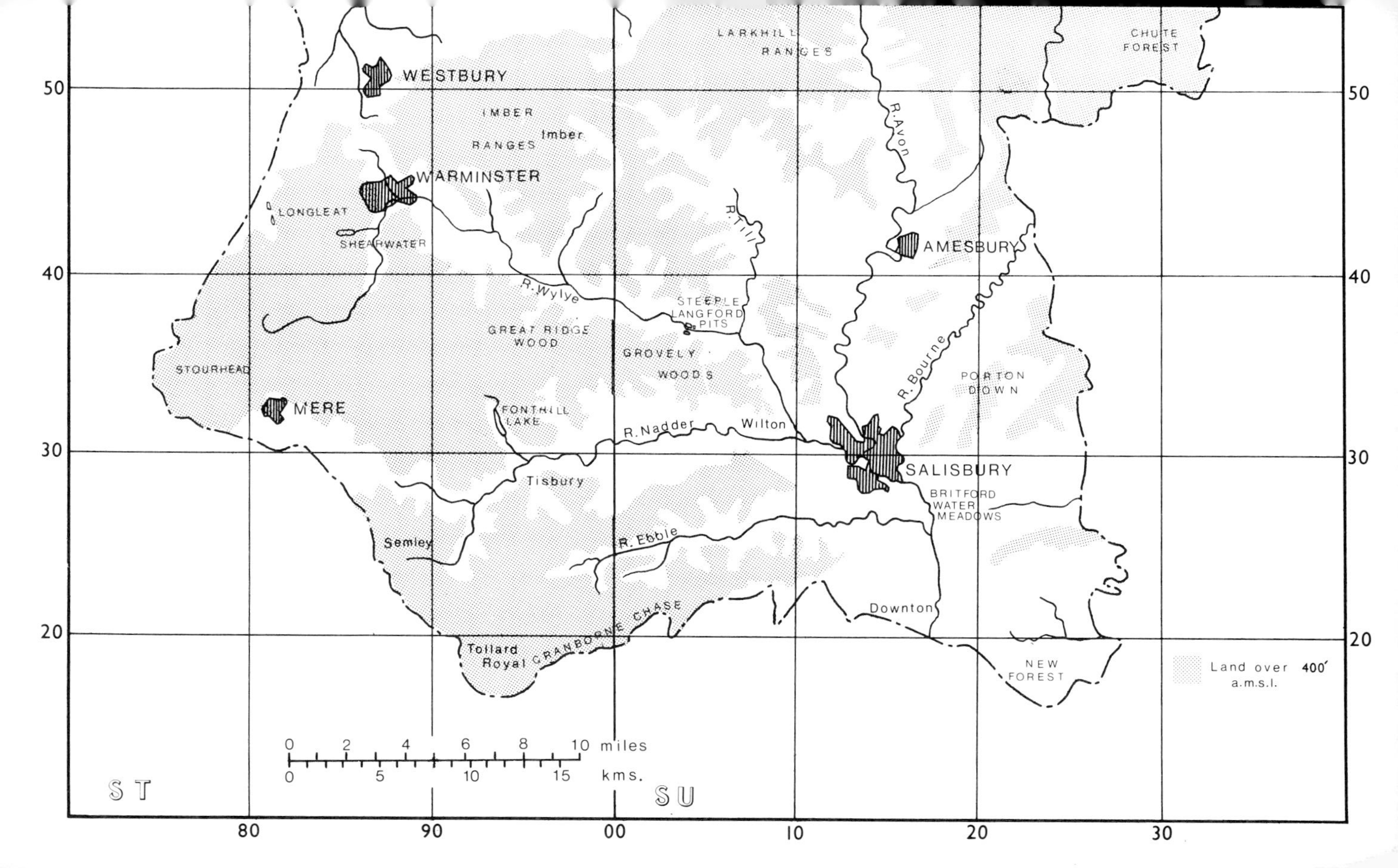

WESTBURY
IMBER RANGES
Imber
WARMINSTER
LONGLEAT
SHEARWATER
STOURHEAD
MERE
LARKHILL RANGES
CHUTE FOREST
R. Avon
R. Till
AMESBURY
R. Wylye
STEEPLE LANGFORD PITS
GREAT RIDGE WOOD
GROVELY WOODS
R. Bourne
PORTON DOWN
FONTHILL LAKE
R. Nadder
Wilton
SALISBURY
BRITFORD WATER MEADOWS
Tisbury
Semley
R. Ebble
CRANBORNE CHASE
Tollard Royal
Downton
NEW FOREST
Land over 400′ a.m.s.l.
0 2 4 6 8 10 miles
0 5 10 15 kms.
ST
SU
80
90
00
10
20
30
40
50